Introduction

As long as man has sought to explore and conquer there has been a need for landing craft. From ancient Persia to the Dardanelles, small boats, often impressed from civilian owners, were used to carry out seaborne raids and invasions. Experimentation and refinement of seaborne assets grew between the First and Second World Wars as their value as strategic assets was reassessed. The United States Navy and Marine Corps in particular looked at how best to utilize and manage what is the most ambitious and complex of all the combined military operations.

By the mid-1930s specifically designed craft were slowly appearing in naval rosters, taking over from naval lighters. Like the lighters, these specialist craft were used to transport cargo and passengers from ship to shore and featured unique flat-bottomed or spoon-billed hulls. In the years leading up to the Second World War, an epoch of purpose-built landing craft and amphibians led by pre-war America in particular took place. The business of producing the perfect landing craft as well as the new concept of the amphibian became a race of applying new technology. All the while, the military began looking at how best to ally the new craft to successful doctrine and tactical development that inevitably followed.

These new ways of thinking, coupled with ever-advancing technological developments, meant that the landing craft became more than a simple low-silhouetted lighter or barge. It had to deliver, protect and defend its load, crew and itself from attack. Alongside the landing craft grew a veritable army of tracked and wheeled amphibians that would come ashore providing direct fire support, delivering logistics and removing the wounded.

Surprisingly the amphibian was not a new concept and had been in use since the 1870 with the advent of the *Alligator* tug. This was a logging vessel manufactured by West & Peachey of Ontario, Canada that would use a chain to pull itself from water body to water body. Whilst not a true amphibian in the contemporary sense of the word, it proved the concept was feasible and as such it was developed from the late 1930s. By the end of the Second World War there several key amphibians in service with all the major belligerents.

After the war, new alliances, technologies and doctrines were shaped and the concepts mapped out in the Second World War further developed. The biggest for seaborne assault was by far the hovercraft, or

A DUKW amphibious truck with a load of medical supplies and personnel moves inland in the southern France invasion area on 26 August 1944, 11 days after the initial assault. USS *LCI(L)-18* is beached in the centre background. Note the Amphibious Forces insignia painted on the side of the DUKW. (NARA)

An iconic image: an LCVP from the U.S. Coast Guard-manned USS *Samuel Chase* disembarks troops of Company E, 16th Infantry Regiment, 1st Infantry Division who are wading onto the Fox Green section of Omaha Beach on the morning of 6 June 1944. On landing, American soldiers encountered the newly formed German 352nd Division, and two-thirds of Company E became casualties. (CPHoM Robert F. Sargent)

Above: An LCM-8 is launched from the well deck of the Amphibious Assault Ship USS *Saipan* (LHA-2) during NATO exercise Display Determination '81. (NARA)

Right: RAF Regiment unloading 20mm guns from an LCT during landings at Rangoon. (IWM)

Right: The SS *River Clyde* beached at Cape Helles, Gallipoli, 1915. (HMSO)

Landing Craft, Air Cushioned (LCAC) with the Soviets fielding the huge 'Zubr'-class hovercraft as the zenith of the concept.

For the modeller, landing craft and amphibians represent a font of inspiration and opportunity, as well as the possibility of producing some wonderful camouflage finishes. From sun-baked beaches of the Pacific to dioramas taking place in the waterways of Central Europe to action-packed, sea-based vignettes, landing craft and amphibians provide the foundation for some wonderfully creative modelling ideas. Some of the vehicles, such as the M113, included in this LandCraft title, have their own books so do refer to these for further reference.

Design and Development

Allied Landing Craft

On 9 January 1916, the last of the Allied troops left the Gallipoli Peninsula as part of a failed campaign to gain control of the Dardanelles, and open a sea lane to the Black Sea. Whilst the tactical and policy questions regarding the failure of the Dardanelles Campaign are beyond the scope of this book, a key part of the campaign's failure was the poor availability of suitable landing craft.

On 25 April 1915, Allied troops approached the shores of the Gallipoli Peninsula in requisitioned civil and merchant vessels, including the SS *River Clyde*. The SS *River Clyde* had been subjected to rudimentary changes to make her a viable military vessel, including the cutting of sally ports into the sides of her hull, which would allow the disembarkation of 2,000 men from the Royal Hampshire Regiment, the Royal Munster Fusiliers and the Royal Dublin Fusiliers onto the landing site. The plan was to beach the SS *River Clyde* with the men then leaving via the sally ports and gangways hung alongside. They would then make their way across walkways thrown over lifeboats and lighters before scrambling ashore. For its own protection and to provide fire support, the SS *River Clyde* was equipped with no less than 11 machine guns positioned in her bow, protected by repurposed boiler steel and sand bags.

On paper the plan was feasible and later landing craft, especially the Landing Craft, Infantry (LCI), would feature some of the innovations the SS *River Clyde* adopted, including hull-mounted gangways for egress. As it was the SS *River Clyde* became a deathtrap for the disembarking troops. On beaching she attracted murderous fire from Turkish positions at Sedd el Bahr castle, and initial attempts to establish a beachhead were unsuccessful. Eventfully a beachhead was established under the cover of darkness; the SS *River Clyde* would remain beached, serving as both a quay and field dressing station. Elsewhere landings had been made via lighters and large unprotected rowing boats.

There was one noticeable success in the Allied campaign and that was the 'X' Lighter which had been commissioned by Admiral Lord Fisher in February 1915. Designed by Walter Pollock of the shipbuilders James Pollock & Son, who subsequently built the new vessels, the 'X' Lighter had been designed in less than a week. The key feature of the new craft was a shallow-draft, spoonbill-shaped hull that could take advantage of steep-shelved beaches, whilst unloading was facilitated by a centrally mounted bow ramp. Powered by a Bolinder heavy oil engine, the 'X' Lighter could also carry a machine-gun mount. Two types were produced by Pollock and other barge builders: the 'K', which was used for troop and horse carriage, and the 'L', for water carriage.

The chaos of war: an array of lighters at Cape Helles, Gallipoli, seen from the bow of the collier SS *River Clyde*. (AWM)

Painted black, the 'X' Lighters soon earned the nickname of 'Black Beetles' and once delivered were extremely successful in their role. After Gallipoli the 'X' Lighter was considered a suitable carrier for the new tank, though nothing came of that idea. After the war most 'X' Lighters would be sold to shipping agents and overseas buyers, though some would continue to serve the military in theatres including the North Russian Campaign of 1919, and the Spanish Civil War. The 'X' Lighters' finest hour would come with Operation Dynamo in 1940, where five of these venerable craft would assist in the evacuation of Allied troops from Dunkirk, in northern France.

By the early 1920s the British had refined their ideas and the Motor Landing Craft (MLC) was developed for the ship-to-shore transport of personnel and stores as well as a medium tank. The MLC came as the result of an inter-service committee which had been brought together to design a craft that met the needs of the army and

Royal Navy (RN). By 1926 the first prototype, designed by shipbuilders J. Samuel White of Cowes, was put forward for trials. Like its predecessor the 'X' Lighter, the box-shaped MLC took on the appearance of the landing craft we're familiar with today, and featured a shallow draft. It was fitted with a Hotchkiss petrol engine which powered a rudimentary directional water jet which would make manoeuvring in shallow waters far easier than propellers, as well as reducing the risk of fouling. The MLC was designed to be carried via ship derrick, which would first lower the MLC, then its cargo. The MLC would then deploy in the traditional manner and was able to cruise at around 5 knots. Upon reaching shore, a bow ramp would be lowered, allowing the deployment of the load. A wonderful exercise in ingenuity and a quantum step forward in maritime architecture, only nine MLCs would be produced and used by the Royal Navy. Sadly, all of these innovative craft would be lost during the course of the Second World War.

Almost simultaneously, the United Sates had begun to consider its own options in terms of seaborne operations and were developing the necessary organizations and arms to facilitate these. Unlike the British, the United States took their seaborne forces development a little more seriously, especially given the need to protect its territories in the Pacific, such as Hawaii and the Philippines. The need for a flexible strategic seaborne approach was recognized and by the end of 1933 the Fleet Marine Force (FMF) had been established.

The Fleet Marine Force, a formalized seaborne force still in existence today, combines the tactical expertise and equipment of United States Marine Corps (USMC) units under the command and control of Navy Fleet commanders. This is then split into Atlantic and Pacific commands with units organized into components known as Marine Air Ground Task Forces (MAGTFs). These can either be deployed as part of naval expeditionary forces or separately as part of larger joint or combined forces supported by a host of sub- and attached units.

As part of the FMF's training and build-up, a series of seven exercises called Fleet Landing Exercise (FLEX) were held between 1935 and 1941 to help shape practical form and doctrine. These helped to define what equipment and tactics worked and what didn't and to then develop solutions to those elements that did not work. As a result, numerous milestones were reached starting with FLEX 1 which immediately identified that the design of both landing craft and boat used by the Marines needed vast improvement. By FLEX 3 the landing craft were being tested to their limits, and in some cases found wanting, meanwhile new techniques were being practised, including the use of cargo netting as a scramble net to aid embarkation.

To further aid support, FLEX 3 saw the introduction of First World War destroyer-converted high-speed transports capable of carrying up to 200 personnel, 40 tons of cargo and providing fire support from their not inconsiderable weapons fit. Known as high-speed transports, or APDs ('AP' for transport and 'D' for destroyer) these re-roled destroyers would initially carry four davit-mounted Landing Craft Personnel, Large (LCP(L)s). These would later be replaced by the more familiar bow-ramped Landing Craft Personnel, Ramped (LCP(R)) or Landing Craft, Vehicle (LCV). The APDs would see extensive service in the Pacific theatre where they performed brilliantly, proving their worth time and again in a range of roles, including mail carriers, anti-submarine warfare vessels and minesweepers.

By FLEX 4 the landing craft issue remained unsolved and so FLEX 5 saw the testing of a range of commercially available boats. These included an adapted Eureka tugboat, a spoonbill-hulled boat made by New Orleans-based boat builder Eureka Tug-Boat Company and adapted by their boat designer and builder, Andrew Higgins.

APD-63 in profile. Notice the early LCP(R) ready for deployment via the overhead davits. (NARA)

Under new management: a captured Japanese Dai Hatsu landing craft showing its unique bow design. (Thomas Fisher)

Above: LCP(L) at Inveraray, Scotland, October 1942. (IWM)

The Higgins-adapted Eureka boat would come to be known as the Landing Craft Personnel, Large (LCP(L)). On test it performed well, though unlike the British MLC and, more worryingly, the recently observed Japanese Dai Hatsu-class landing craft, it lacked a bow ramp. This meant that personnel were exposed to enemy fire when alighting, but this issue was soon overcome by the addition of a retractable bow ramp.

Based on a model originally developed in 1924, the Dai Hatsu-class landing craft was first adopted by the Imperial Japanese Army (IJA). After further refinement the landing craft was adopted by the Imperial Japanese Navy (IJN) and used by the IJA in the 1932 Shanghai Incident to land troops to block Chinese supply lines. US Naval Intelligence had been observing the development of Japanese seaborne tactics and equipment and as a result were able to furnish Higgins with photographs and information, including the use of a lowering bow ramp that would help shape the designs of the LCP(L), LCP(R) and LCV.

The LCP(L) may not have been as seaworthy as the Dai Hatsu, but it had had to hit the ground running and without the luxury of eight years of design and development that the Dai Hatsu had received. If anything, the LCP(L) showed just how inspired Higgins's adaption of his Eureka boat design was. The Eureka handled as well on the water as it did in the shallows thanks to its 1.05m (3ft 6in) draft, and was fully capable of beaching and subsequent self-recovery should the need arise – a trick that had been exceptionally useful for commercial loggers for whose use it had originally been designed.

The LCP(L) was a mix of pine and plywood construction and featured sections of metal armour plating. It was capable of transporting a platoon, which could be loaded whilst the LCP(L) was still attached to its davits, or, for follow-up troops, over the side via a suspended cargo net. The LCP(L) also attracted the interest of the British Admiralty who would make an initial purchase of 136 craft from Higgins in October 1940.

In the water the LCP(L) had a three-man crew, a coxswain and two gunners, who were drawn either from the United States Navy (USN) or United States Coast Guard (USCG). In the Royal Navy boat crews would be either sailors or Royal Marines. Regardless of rank, the coxswain maintained overall command of the vessel and the two gunners were responsible for other duties with one also acting as engineer and the other as bowman. This arrangement would also be used in the LCP(R) and LCV. The two gunners were positioned at the bow with the coxswain behind the port side gunner's positions.

The LCP(L)s were fitted with a range of both petrol and diesel engines during the production period with USN and USMC LCP(L)s capable of producing a speed of 8 knots whilst Royal Navy versions were capable of 11 knots. Whilst predominantly a ship-to-shore craft, the LCP(L) could also be towed within range of its beaching site before being cast off. This method was used for a series of commando raids by the British in Northern Europe throughout the Second World War, most notably the ill-fated raid on the French coastal town of Dieppe.

An LCP(R) swings precariously overhead whilst Marines of the 1st Marine Division embark for Korea aboard USS *Henrico*, San Diego, 13 July 1950. (USN)

The Landing Craft Personnel, Ramped (LCP(R)) was a development of the LCP(L) made in 1942 by the USN's Bureau of Construction and Repair. This featured a small ramp cut into the bow between the gunner's positions which could then be lowered, along with a section of the forward armoured bulkhead to allow for troop egress. Not only did this change protect disembarking troops, but it also greatly reduced the time needed to unload. Whilst other developments would overshadow the LCP(R), it was nevertheless an important step in refining the landing craft's design. Given it would see limited service and be overshadowed by the Landing Craft, Vehicle (LCV), it would continue to provide vital support as a logistic vessel. The LCP(R) retained the three-man crew and range of powerplants found in the LCP(L).

The next major step change in the development of the Landing Craft, Vehicle (LCV) was another Higgins design. Higgins had privately developed three craft specifically designed to carry vehicles and in 1941 the USMC Equipment Board ordered one such craft to be modified to fit a 1,900mm- (6ft 3in-) wide ramp, As well as the ramp, three craft were ordered with varying drives: two featured straight drives whilst a third was fitted with a dual driveshaft known as a V-drive.

Unforeseen role: an LCV minesweeper underway; this was Britain's smallest minesweeper of the Second World War. The LCV's shallow draft was invaluable for minesweeping in shallow water. (IWM)

Troops land at Omaha Beach, 6 June 1944. Note DUKWs and halftracks at the water line, as well as the advancing troops heading inland. (NARA)

The specification also laid out the load space with one straight-drive craft having 5.5m (17ft 8in) cargo space and the other having 5.9m (19ft 3in) cargo space. The latter was chosen as the more successful and in March 1942, it was accepted into service as the LCV. Its first major test would the Operation Torch landing in November 1942 and an improved version known as the Landing Craft, Vehicle and Personnel (LCVP) would go on to be chosen as the standard landing craft for the US. Like the LCP(L) and LCP(R), the LCVP would have a three-man crew and could carry a platoon of troops, or 5 tons (11,000lb) of cargo.

The Landing Craft, Vehicle and Personnel (LCVP) was the ultimate expression of Higgins's design, prompting no less a personality than General Dwight Eisenhower to proclaim, 'Andrew Higgins is the man who won the war for us.' The LCVP, like its predecessors, was made from plywood with a steel ramp and was crewed by four, a stern man now being added to the crew roster. The LCVP featured a wider well deck of 2,29mm (7ft 8in), though this was shorter in length than the LCV by 7.5mm (3in). Other refinements included over a ton of side and bow armour and the coxswain moved to a more sheltered position inside the boat. Another key design feature was the ability to stack LCVPs on their davits, thus allowing larger ships to carry more boats.

For all these refinements the LCVP had two drawbacks: the first was its inability to traverse corals and shallow water, which often excluded its use in the Pacific theatre where Landing Vehicle, Tracked (LVT) and Landing Craft, Mechanized (LCM) would fill the gap. The second was the LCVP's weight, a hefty 8,100kg (17,800lb), but this did not prevent over 23,000 boats being built.

By the time FLEX 6 took place in 1940 it presented the FMF with an opportunity to field a force of two tank and two artillery lighters, twenty-five special landing craft including 17 LCP(L)s and eight landing skiffs. Also included were five Landing Craft, Rubber boats (LCRs). FLEX 7 was the final exercise, where the FMF was able to hone its skills in both day and night attacks.

Whilst the FMF's concept development was cut short by the US's entry into the war, the FLEX exercises had given the USMC in particular an edge, and more importantly usable landing craft. Across the Atlantic the British had eagerly been watching developments in the United States and by 1939 had developed the Landing Craft, Assault (LCA) which followed in the wake of the Motor Landing Craft (MLC)

Like the Americans the British were keenly aware of their lack of seaborne assets. The challenges of depression austerity, increasingly sophisticated air power assets and the disaster of the Dardanelles left a reticence to develop specialist landing craft. By the 1930s, the European political scene had shifted considerably with the rise of fascism and the subsequent rearmament programmes. Once again Britain was forced to review its defence stance and offensive capabilities, and in 1938 Major-General Bernard Montgomery held a combined seaborne exercise involving troops from the 3rd Division making a beach landing at Slapton Sands, Devon. (Slapton Sands would later become the site of the infamous E-boat ambush and subsequent friendly fire incidents which marred Exercise Tiger, a major pre-invasion exercise, that saw over 1,200 American servicemen lose their life.)

Montgomery's exercise, supported by Royal Navy strike aircraft, showed that the seaborne assault was as relevant as ever; it also showed that landing by naval cutter was impracticable which highlighted the need for a domestically mass-produced landing craft. Another equally important development, echoing developments across the Atlantic, was the establishment of doctrine by the Inter-Service Training and Development Centre (ISTDC) for the use of landing craft. Given that the current in-service landing craft, the MLC, had been in service for almost a decade, this seemed almost ludicrous. However, weaknesses had been detected in time and new landing craft would be designed to complement seaborne assault doctrine.

The specifications for the new landing craft were straightforward enough: the new landing craft would have to weigh less than 10 tons to allow handling by passenger liner davits. The craft's design would focus on taking its payload from ship to shore and landing them in water at a depth no greater than 450mm (18in). At the same time, a separate set of requirements was laid down for a larger and dedicated vehicle and supplies landing craft, the Landing Craft, Mechanized (LCM).

Due to the current surge of rearmament the Royal Navy was undertaking, the Director of Naval Construction (DNC), who was busy designing new ships, felt that the task of designing new landing craft was not a particularly vital one. The ISTDC, understandably feeling the opposite, approached the Board of Trade for suggestions around a suitable maritime architect.

An initial LCA design, known as the Fleming craft, was built from the aluminium alloy Birmabright, by J. Samuel Wright of Cowes, Isle of Wright, and thoroughly tested by the ISTDC before being presented to the DNC for final assessment. The assessment was less than complimentary, but the DNC accepted the need for further trials, including landing trials which the ISTDC had planned in the coming months. At the same time the DNC asked for, and received, the ISTDC landing craft specifications to enable the external tender of alternative designs that might prove superior to the Fleming craft. Of the three companies approached by the DNC, only one, John I. Thornycroft & Company, responded, and provided a design in 48 hours.

One way to refuel. An LCM loaded with a bowser refuels A Short Sunderland GR Mk V of No. 205 Squadron RAF Detachment, moored off Direction Island, Cocos Islands. (IWM)

LCA-1377 ferries American troops during preparations for D-Day. (US Army)

A subsequent review of the design by both the DNC and the ISTDC led to the construction of a prototype being approved for experimental purposes on the understanding that the DNC held no responsibility. Unlike the metal-hulled Fleming craft, the Thornycroft design was given a hull of mahogany and powered by two 65hp Ford V8 engines (which gave the LCA a top speed of 6 knots), as opposed to the Fleming craft's two 120hp Chrysler engines.

Both craft were sent to Langstone harbour, Hampshire, for competitive trials where the Fleming craft was deemed the more favourable given its low silhouette and ease of disembarking as well as having a more efficient passage in water. However, it was also loud, due to the hull acting as an amplifier for the two engines, so that any tactical surprise would be lost. Another issue lay in the Birmabright chemical compounding and shape that made the addition of appliqué armour impossible.

On the other hand, any issues that the Thornycroft craft had could all be overcome; a second prototype featured a

A wonderful view of a factory-fresh LCA being launched in the summer of 1942. (RN)

LCI used for D-Day training. (Unknown)

double-diagonal mahogany hull, which could be armoured. Along with a lower silhouette, the engines could be silenced so effectively that they could not being heard at a distance of 23m (75ft 5in). The Thornycroft craft also produced a small bow wave and, most importantly, with its spoon-billed hull, it could be easily beached. All design aspects made for a craft that could make stealthy landings, though its narrow ramp and subsequent slow disembarkation time remained an Achilles heel.

So, despite the Fleming craft's success at trials, it was the Thornycroft craft which was chosen as the successful design by the DNC. Consequently, the Admiralty provided an initial order of 18 of the new LCAs from Thornycroft in April 1939 with a further eight ordered in September.

With a crew of four, coxswain, two seaman and a stoker, the LCAs featured flush-decked hulls capable of carrying up 36 troops in its long central section with benches fitted port, centre and starboard. To the front was a split armoured bulkhead which swung outwards allowing access to the ramp which was deployed via pulleys and wire. The ramp itself featured rollers on its leading edge to prevent it digging in on beaching and to allow some movement when grounded. Well-drilled troops could exit the LCA via the ramp in around two and a half minutes.

By the side of the forward bulkhead was a starboard-located roofless pilot house, surrounded on three sides by 60cm-(24in-) high armour plate above the deck line. Opposite sat the Lewis gun position, which would receive armour later on in the production run. Behind the central cargo was the realm of the stoker and the sternsheetsman, engines and control mechanisms.

The LCA's crew of four were highly trained and came from either the Royal Navy and as the war progressed, the Royal Marines. As well as the coxswain, who controlled the rudders and commanded the LCA, there was the bowman/gunner whose tasks included opening and closing the split bulkhead doors, as well as raising and lowering the ramp. Alongside the stoker, who was responsible for engine compartment and engine control, guided by the coxswain via voice pipe and telegraph, was the sternsheetsman. The sternsheetsman's task was to assist in lowering and raising the boat at the davits of the Landing Ship, Infantry (LSI).

Should the coxswain or stoker be incapacitated, either the sternsheetsman and bowman was able to take over, a useful skill when employed on longer journeys that allowed the crew to take alternate rest periods. To help maintain a pool of suitably trained crews in the early days of use, the Royal Navy established Combined Operations naval base, HMS *Quebec*, at Inveraray, Scotland, where crews were retained and trained until needed for operations.

The LCA, like the LCVP, was constructed from wood with the sides protected with 10lb DIHT armour, a heat-treated tooling steel, and by 1942 deck armour began to make an appearance. The buoyancy material Onazote was used extensively throughout, filling the bow section between the armoured doors and the ramp. Each bulkhead void was also filled as well as both sides of the hull for the length of the well, along with part of the aft compartment. Either side of the hull on the upper surfaces was storage for the canvas hold covers, scaling ladders and other necessary equipment.

The Admiralty placed further orders for 30 units in March 1940 by which time Thornycroft was subcontracting the task to a range of South Coast yacht-builders whilst they concentrated on constructing War Emergency Programme destroyers. By mid-1941, the order process had become refined, with the Admiralty ordering LCAs directly from cabinetmakers, carpenters and boat builders throughout the United Kingdom. Slowly production increased and by the eve of Operation *Overlord*, LCA production was around 60 units a month. In total over 2,000 LCAs were built between 1939 and 1945.

Alongside the LCA, Thornycroft began development of the Landing Craft Mechanized Mk 1 (LCM(1)), a larger logistics support craft with a load capacity of 16 tons and designed primarily for the transportation of armour from ship to shore. Unlike the LCA, the LCM(1), initially referred to as 'Landing Barge', was of all-steel construction with armour plate, and, much like its smaller cousin, could beach in as little as 40cm (1ft 4in) of water and move in the water marginally faster at 7 knots. Crewed by six; coxswain, stoker, and four seamen, the LCM(1) was capable of being deployed with its load via carrier vessel davits, or deployed unloaded, with the load added after the LCM(1) was in the water. Early LCM(1)s were powered by two Thornycroft 60bhp petrol engines, which eventually gave way to Chrysler 6-cylinder in-line types, again producing 60bhp.

By the autumn of 1940, the LCM(1) had taken over most of the roles previously fulfilled by the MLC fleet, which had suffered heavy losses at the Battle of Narvik and during Operation Dynamo. Now the primary logistics landing craft for the Royal Navy, the LCM(1) remained at the forefront of supply missions until the arrival of the many US-made LCMs and their vaiants. Built between 1938 and 1944, Thornycroft and their sub-contractors made around 500 LCM(1)s.

The LCM concept proved to be exceptionally popular with the USMC, especially when their interest in light tanks waned in favour of the far more practical and heavier medium tank designs that were now appearing. At this point the USN Bureau of Construction and Repair started to review a series of designs, some of which, even though bought, were wholly unsuitable. As a result, the bureau once again approached Higgins and in 1941 he began the development of a suitable design. Initially a 13.7m (45ft) design was offered, but this was later increased to 15.3m (50ft), to help cope with increased weight of the latest M4 tank. These LCMs could also carry up to 60 troops, which would be essential as the war progressed.

Meanwhile, the United States Bureau of Ships had designed their own 13.7m (45ft) LCM, which they felt was on a par with that produced by Higgins. However, a comparative sea trial was arranged to check the capability of both designs in landing a tank. The bureau design almost floundered and failed to land the tank, and the USN staff overseeing the trail agreed the Higgins design was superior to their own. Higgins was awarded the contract to produce his design alongside the bureau's own design.

The bureau's design was referred to as LCM(2), and was the first to see service in the Mediterranean and Pacific whilst the 15.3m (50ft) Higgins design, LCM(3), would see service in North Africa. As the war progressed and the weight of armoured fighting vehicles increased, so too did the design of the LCM family with LCM(6) lengthened by 1.8m (6ft) amidships. At the same time the Royal Navy continued to develop their LCM fleet and these developments became known as LCM(4), (5) and (7) among the Allies.

A row of newly completed LCM(3) tank lighters sitting at a US naval drydock after production-line completion. NARA

An early TLC, seen here with a Crusader I tank, testing a portable concrete roadway. IWM

At the same time the LCM was realized, a parallel project was underway, the Tank Landing Craft (TLC), later changed to Landing Craft, Tank (LCT). The LCT became the next step in the evolution of the landing craft design process, led once again by the Royal Navy on the insistence of wartime Prime Minister Winston Churchill. The LCT would be a specially designed craft that was strong and big enough to transport three 36-ton armoured fighting vehicles for ship-to-shore and shore-to-shore support operations. In the spirit of previous landing craft, it would be inexpensive to construct and have the ability to sustain itself at sea for a week.

The initial design by the maritime architect Sir Roland Baker, a man whose reputation matched that of Higgins, had been drafted in three days after a request from Captain Loben Maund, commandant of the Inter-Service Training and Development Centre. At the time, Baker was superintendent of landing craft, working under Lord Mountbatten and was perfectly placed to design such a craft. The initial design was of a 46m (152ft) landing craft with an 8.8m (29ft) beam and a shallow draft. The details of the design were then finessed by shipbuilders Fairfields and

John Brown under the guidance of the Admiralty Experimental Works at Haslar. The first landing craft, Mark 1, delivering a speed of 10 knots, was built by Tyneside shipbuilding company R. & W. Hawthorn, Leslie & Company, Limited. Overall, 30 Mark 1s were built by the end of 1940.

The LCT was a 372-ton steel-hulled vessel that drew a remarkable 0.91m (3ft) of water at the bow. It featured a 3.7m- (12ft-) wide hinged ramp that enabled tanks to exit directly onto the beaches, similar in style to the LCM craft, while a second steel door behind the ramp sealed the bow area from the tank deck. Along the hull sides the watertight bulwark coamings contained storage compartments added to the buoyancy provided by the double bottom beneath the main tank deck. The double-bottom hull also contained the ballast and fuel tanks which contained enough fuel for a range of 900 nautical miles (1,700km or 1,000 miles). They were also designed to allow the fore and aft trim to be adjusted for beaching.

The bridge was located at the stern, underneath which sat the two 350hp Hall-Scott petrol engines, along with an auxiliary generator, batteries and pumps. Aft of the engine room were quarters for ten crewmen with galley and storage. Behind the bridge was a wardroom for two officers, and mounts for port and starboard 2-pounder pom-pom guns.

The key component to the success of the LCT's operation was the large stern-mounted kedge anchor, which was dropped three to four ship lengths from shore and used as a brake. The kedge prevented the LCT from slewing or broaching, and, combined with its powerful winch, gave the LCT the ability to self-extract from any beach once its cargo was unloaded. The bow ramp was initially raised and lowered by a series of hand cranks, but as the war progressed later versions were treated to a powered winch. In subsequent marks, despite the size differences, the basic arrangement of power ramp, long tank well and aft steering station was retained.

German POWs unload a vehicle from an LCT near Ouistreham, France, 11 June 1944. (IWM)

Initial sea trials proved the Mark 1 a challenge to anyone's seamanship, in fact, almost unmanageable in certain conditions. During testing the craft's shallow draft made steering by the helm alone all but impossible, and a quick engine response was essential in preventing calamity. Issues continued below decks with the crew compartment being damp, the sound from the two engines far from comfortable and the engine spaces themselves hot and cramped. Despite these shortcomings, the prototype LCT was able to land tanks on any beach.

By the advent of the Mark 2, the designers had corrected the faults found in the Mark 1, leaving a longer and wider craft powered by either three Paxman diesels or Napier Lion petrol engines. The wheelhouse and gun tubs were treated to 15lb and 20lb armoured shielding. The increased length and beam now allowed two rows of 25-ton tanks to be loaded and enough fuel to triple the range to 2,700 nautical miles (5,000km or 3,100 miles). In terms of handling and reliability, the Mark 2 was a vast improvement on the Mark 1.

The growth of the type continued with the Mark 3 being treated to an additional 9.8m (32ft) midsection that gave it an overall length of 59m (192ft) and a displacement of 640 tons. The increased length allowed the Mark 3 to carry five 40-ton tanks and all their related support equipment, or 300 tons of deck cargo. Though the Royal Navy appreciated the higher load capacity of the Mark 3, the rush to get the craft into service meant that insufficient testing had taken place. This would lead to the need to add longitudinal stiffeners to avoid tensional stress to the hull.

The Mark 4 was slightly shorter and lighter than the Mark 3, but with a wider beam of 11.8m (38ft 9in) and was designed specifically for cross-Channel work. The widening of the hull also allowed for improved accommodation for tank crews. Its displacement of 586 tons was powered along by two 460hp Paxman diesels. With a capacity of 350 tons, it could carry a remarkable load of nine M4 Sherman or six Churchill tanks. Its use in the Dieppe raid highlighted a lack of manoeuvring ability which identified the need to shorten the hull further. At this point in the war, most LCTs would be built by a range of contractors in the United States, starting with the Mark 5.

With the United States' entry into the war, some elements of its landing craft were missing and the LCT filled a rather wide gap, so they drew on British designs for assistance and inspiration. One of these was a double-ended LCT intended to work with landing ships and designed by K. C. Barnaby of Thornycroft. The Bureau of Ships quickly adapted Barnaby's plans, designing a craft with a single ramp and

286-ton displacement. The design had a crew of 12 and one officer and was 35.7m (117ft) long with a 9.8m (32ft) beam capable of accommodating four 40-ton tanks or 150 tons of cargo. Powered by three 225hp Gray marine diesels which gave the Mark 5 a top speed of 8 knots, and a range if just 700 nautical miles (1,300km or 810 miles). Though never designed to cross the Pacific under their own steam, so to speak, several flotillas of LCTs did make the journey from Pearl Harbor to forward areas. They could also be towed to areas of operation by larger vessels such as the Landing Ship, Dock (LSD), and once there they could cross the short distances between islands under their own power.

An ingenious aspect of the design was its ability to be shipped in three watertight pieces on either a cargo ship or carried as an assembled craft aboard a Landing Ship, Tank (LST). This meant the LCT could be assembled in the water or launched by tilting the LST on its beam and letting the LCT simply slide, fully laden, into the water. The Mark 6 had the same engines, equipment and crew as the Mark 5, but was slightly longer, at 36.6m (120ft).

The main difference between the Mark 5 and 6 was the addition of a stern gate that allowed the Mark 6 to moor in front of larger LSTs, thus becoming a bridge for tanks and vehicles disembarking the deeper-draft vessel. Whilst a clever bit of engineering in practice, the act was far more complex, especially in the Pacific theatre where the strong tidal currents and uncharted reef shoals limited the beaching of heavy armoured vehicles.

When the system was employed, the LCT came into its own; its small wheelhouse was moved to the starboard side of the 4.27m- (14ft) wide passage that enable the system to work.

The Mark 6 was a rugged craft and it was this aspect that naval architects wanted to exploit in designing the Mark 7, which would have troop-carrying accommodation that the Mark 6 lacked. As the design of the Mark 7 was heavily influenced by operational experience in the Pacific theatre, it found itself redesignated as Landing Ship, Medium (LSM).

The final LCT design was the British Mark 8, capable of carrying eight heavy tanks or 350 tons of cargo, as well as featuring accommodation for 50 troops alongside a crew of 22. This was the final expression of the LCT, though sadly it was too late to see service in the Second World War; it would, however, give sterling service post-war.

Like the LCT, the Landing Craft Infantry, Large (LCI(L)) was a shore-to-shore craft designed to land up to 200 personnel directly onto beaches. The LCI(L) was developed in response to a request made by Vice-Admiral Lord Mountbatten, commander of Combined Operations, who wanted a craft capable of carrying and landing a large body of troops. As the steel to make the hull was already earmarked for destroyer construction in the United Kingdom, the USN Bureau of Ships and its chief of Preliminary Design, Captain Edward Cochrane, was approached to help build the new craft. Cochrane was a highly capable and experienced naval architect, holding a Master of Science degree from the Massachusetts Institute of Technology (MIT) and his experience would prove invaluable in shaping the design.

The father of the modern commandos, Lord Louis Mountbatten (right), watching a landing exercise on the beach at the Combined Operations centre at Dundonald Camp. Note the dummy LCA's ramp leading into a water pit to simulate an amphibious landing. (IWM)

Mountbatten's initial intention had been to build a somewhat frugal craft that was expendable after a single trip. The design developed when it was realized that in some cases troop transportation would take place over longer distances than simply cross-Channel and suitable accommodation was required. Cochrane quickly designed a craft that was easily built featuring a mass-produced design that utilized non-traditional shipbuilding facilities and equipment.

The design featured three key variants which shared a common hull 48m (158ft) long, with a 7m (23ft) beam, with differing positions for their ramps and the shapes of the conning towers. Variant 1 featured a square conning tower and side ramps, and was the original style design of LCI(L). The second variant featured a round conning tower and side ramps, and the final variant a round conning tower and bow ramp. The round conning tower was a change that gave crews better visibility than the square type originally fitted. The two variants fitted with side ramps featured a deck which was wider than the prow with two gangways on either side of the bow, which in turn led onto a pair of ramps that could be lowered to allow for troop disembarkation. The narrowness of the ramps often led to troops being thrown over the side whilst disembarking, and it also exposed them to enemy fire. As a result, the LCI(L) was intended to be used after the initial assault on an objective by LCAs or LCP(L) s. The bow ramp type got around this issue by utilizing the enclosed ramp and bow doors arrangement similar to the LCT, thus offer disembarking troops more protection. Like the LCT all versions featured a stern-mounted kedge anchor as well, which, like

Semaphore instructions being signalled to *LCI(L) 124* and an LCT during the invasion of Sicily, 10 July 1943. (IWM)

The last of a proud line: former Signalman 3rd Class Gilbert Nadeau and Royal Thai Navy Lt Sathaporn Thassanaleelaporn raise the flag on USS *LCS(L) 102*, the last remaining ship of the landing craft support (large) class, 10 November 2007. (USN)

the LCT, would be used to pull the LCI(L) away from its position on the shoreline.

LCI(L)s were twin-shaft propelled by eight Detroit Diesel 6-71 engines generating 1,600bhp giving the LCI(L) a top speed of 16 knots. The engines were arranged in two banks of four, together using individual drive clutches, with each bank powering a propeller shaft. This arrangement also allowed for an unserviceable engine to be disconnected and repaired whilst leaving the remaining three to power the craft. For internal power the LCI(L) featured two auxiliary Detroit Diesel 2-71s driving the two 30kW 120V D.C. ship's service generators. The LCI(L) was manned by three officers and 21 ratings.

For self-protection the LCI(L) was initially armed with up to five Oerlikon 20mm cannons, each mounted inside a round gun tub with an integral splinter shield. As the war progressed some of the LCI(L) fleet were modified to LCI gunboats, which saw Oelikon cannon removed and replaced with heavier single-barrelled Bofors 40mm guns. Another adaption was the LCI(R) (Rocket) which saw the fitting of rocket-launching racks in place of the side ramps as well as inside the well decks, whilst the LCI(M) was modified to carry three M2 4.2in mortars.

The Landing Craft, Support (Large) Mk 3 (LCS(L)(3)) was a landing craft without which many seaborne operations might have come unstuck as the war progressed. Whilst the LCS(L)(3) wasn't produced in great numbers – only 130 of all variants were produced – she shared a hull design with the Landing Craft, Infantry (LCI). This gave the LCS(L)(3) a length of 48.3m (159ft), a beam of 7.1m (23ft) and a draft of 1.8m (6ft). The hull's flat bottom and skegs between and on either side of the twin propellers allowed the LCS(L)(3) to safely beach in the same manner as the LCI. Like the LCI the LCS(L)(3) used its stern kedge anchor to help pull itself free from the shoreline if necessary.

LCS(L)(3)s could be produced by an experienced yard in as little as ten days, with the final fitting of naval and military equipment taking a few more weeks. LCS(L)(3)s also made excellent firefighting ships with a manifold fitted in front of the bow gun along with two monitors with pumps fitted just forward of the aft gun.

The LCS(L)(3) was fitted with twin variable pitch screws, each powered by a bank of four Grey Marine (later General Motors) diesel engines. All eight engines gave the LCS(L)(3) a total power of 1,600hp along with a maximum speed of 16.5 knots and a cruising speed of 12 knots. The LCS(L)(3) also had a formidable shore-to shore range of 5,500nm (10,200km or 6,050 miles).

The LCS(L)(3) ships positively bristled with weaponry and carried more firepower per ton than any ship ever built for the USN, which earned it the nickname the 'Mighty Midget'. Fitted with three guns and ten rocket launchers as her main armament, the LCS(L)(3) certainly packed a punch. Her bow was fitted with a 3in gun, as well as a single or a twin 40mm gun. The forward and aft deck guns were also twin 40mm. The ten Mark 7 rocket launchers were situated behind the bow gun and forward deckhouse. The LCS(L)(3) also carried four 20mm cannons. The LCS(L)(3) also featured 4.5kg (10lb) STS splinter shields on its gun mounts, pilot house and conning tower as well as an onboard smoke generator which was used to obscure landing craft approaching the beach.

The final vessel that saw extensive use with the Western Allies was the Landing Ship, Tank (LST). Whilst not strictly a craft due to its size, its inclusion here is important as the LST was a huge vessel capable of carrying truly prodigious loads and very much a 'Mother Ship' to other landing craft, including the LCT. Also referred to, somewhat impolitely' as the 'Large Slow Target', the LST was the zenith of the western powers amphibious doctrine.

The initially idea for a large tank-carrying craft came from the Royal Navy's Admiralty who wanted a transatlantic ship known as the Atlantic Tank Landing craft

USS *LST 543* unloading via one of the Mulberry Harbour sections. In the background can be seen Phoenix caissons with anti-aircraft guns. (USN)

(ATL). The design process was started in 1940 with the Admiralty making the first drafts of the 'Atlantic LCT'. Due to political pressure to ensure the concept was sound, the first series of vessels were not built from the keel up, but converted from Maracaibo-class oil tankers.

These had been specifically chosen as they featured a shallow draft, the result of working in Lake Maracaibo in Venezuela, which was awash with sandbars. Three tankers were chosen for conversion: two were 117m (383ft) long, the third slightly shorter. The ships had a varying beam of 1.2m (4ft) forward and 4.6m (15ft) aft. The conversion centred on providing two bow doors and a 30m (100ft) ramp system to allow vehicles to disembark from ship to shore. The ramp was inspired as it allowed the LST to berth on the port side, but also to bypass natural beach obstacles, such as shingle, which would prove disastrous to tanks (as proved at Dieppe). The Maracaibo conversions would also now be known as the Landing Ship, Tank (LST).

By July 1941 the first conversion was completed, with the other two following. The new LSTs could carry 500 tons, which equated to 18 30-ton tanks, or 33 heavy trucks. It could also berth 217 troops and had a crew of 98. Whilst not completely successful, the Maracaibo conversions proved the concept sound and provided the Royal Navy with a useful tool whilst the construction of its first purpose-built LST was underway.

Known initially as 'Winettes', a nod to Churchill's enthusiasm for the project, the new ships became known as the *Boxer* class and were officially designated LST(1). At 122m (400ft) in length they could carry 13 30-ton tanks or 27 heavy trucks as well as 193 troops. The LST(1) was also faster than the *Maracaibo* conversions, capable of 17 knots compared to 10 knots. The issue was that the LST(1) took time to complete with the first ships not available until early 1943. As a result, only three LST(1)s were built as British shipyards were concentrating on the production of escorts and merchant shipping which left the facilities needed to produce the LST(1)s non-existent. Once again the Admiralty turned to the US Navy's Bureau of Ships for assistance in designing and building the next generation of LSTs, the LST(2).

The Admiralty's new design was shared with US counterparts in November 1941 – naval architect John Neidermair drew out a scale plan of the new LST(2) in an afternoon. Neidermair's design was approved, with shipbuilders, the Dravo Corporation, based in Pittsburgh, Pennsylvania, awarded the first construction contract. The first keel was laid in June 1942 and in six months she was completed.

The new LST(2) was 100m (328ft) long, with a 15m (50ft) beam and capable of carrying 2,100 tons of cargo, reduced to 500 tons for beaching operations. The load, which remained the same as the original Maracaibo conversions, this was spread over two decks. These were accessible by ramps on early versions, which were late replaced by an elevator.

As well as having the capacity to carry tanks, the LST(2) was fitted with two to six davits for carrying other landing craft as well as being able to carry an LCT in the upper deck. The crew had swollen in size to 210 and the LST(2) had accommodation for 160 troops.

For protection the LST(2) carried a wide range of ordnance depending on the end user. The USN LST(2)s carried up to seven 40mm and six 20mm guns, whilst RN versions carried a 12-pounder (76.2mm) naval gun and six 20mm guns. Powered by diesel engines, the new LCTs would see action in Northern Europe and the Mediterranean. Some 1,050 LST(2)s were constructed.

American troops crowd the deck as the landing ship tank *LST 25* goes in to unload its cargo of men and trucks between St Laurent and Vierville. (IWM)

A Sherman BARV tows a disabled truck and its load off the beach, Normandy, 14 June 1944. (IWM)

Seen through the open bows of an LST, this Rhino ferry heads for the shore, loaded with wheeled transport, during the early phases of the Normandy landings. (IWM)

Fast food to go Allied style. An LBK is surrounded by various landing craft just off the French coast in the early stages of the D-Day landings. (IWM)

However, accessibility to the new LST(2) by the Royal Navy was hampered by the US, who, rightly so, felt that they should control the numbers released to the RN, given they were producing them. As a result the British returned to producing their own LST, now known as the LST(3). However, the new ship was hampered by the lack of diesel motive power units and welders, which meant the new ships were riveted together and powered by a standard maritime reciprocating steam engine. The LST(3) was larger, had a deeper draft and was slower than the LST(2) with no marked increase in payload.

Overall, the LST series were extremely hardy vessels, capable of absorbing a great deal of battle damage with relatively few losses – a mere 26 were lost to enemy action. As well as carrying tanks, the LST could be converted to fulfil a range of tasks and was capable of carrying locomotives and rolling stock when fitted with tracks, which was a welcome capacity in Northern Europe.

Two other craft in use with the Allies that are worth mentioning are landing barges and the Rhino ferry. Landing barges were British adaptations of Thames barges and lighters as landing craft. In size, they sat between landing craft and landing ships. The barges came in an arrangement of fits including force protection, transportation, supply (food, water and oil) and repair (fitted out with workshops). Some barges were self-powered, while others were towed to the area of operations. Those barges fitted for vehicle carrying had a ramp fitted in place at the rear and unlike the LCT's had to back onto beaches.

The Rhino ferry was a barge constructed by engineers from several pontoons connected together and equipped with outboard engines. The Rhino ferry was used to transport a range of stores from ship to shore and due to their shallow drafts were suited to beach landings. The system could also be used as a pier when filled with water.

The Landing Barge, Kitchen (LBK) was fitted with a large superstructure containing a galley. With a crew of 20-plus, they could carry enough food to feed 800 personnel for a week, providing 1,600 hot and 800 cold meals a day, including freshly baked bread. The smoke produced by the LBK was welcomed by the seamen, as it inadvertently provided a smokescreen for surrounding vessels.

The one asset that was found to be invaluable in assisting grounded landing craft back into the water was the Beach Armoured Recovery Vehicle (BARV). Developed and operated by the Royal Electrical and Mechanical Engineers (REME), the Sherman had been selected for use as it was thought its welded hull would be easier to waterproof than that of other vehicles available. The BARV was diesel powered as it was felt this type of engine would be less affected by the temperature changes caused by the regular ventures into cold water.

Originally a converted and waterproofed Sherman M4A2, the BARV replaced its turret with a pronounced armoured superstructure. The BARV was capable of operating in water up to 2.7m (9ft) deep. Its crew included a trained diver whose job was to attach the necessary towing chains and ropes to stranded vehicles as well as refloating landing craft or removing swamped vehicles from the shoreline. Some 60 BARVs were deployed for use during the invasion of Northern Europe.

To the east the Soviet experience was one of mixed fortunes; given the vast tracts of water that were encompassed by the Soviet Socialist Republics, there seemed little interest in developing a working amphibious doctrine. Both the army and navy were concerned with vast modernization programmes, whilst senior commanders and military thinkers felt it best to keep a low profile in the belligerent domestic political environment.

As a result, the Soviets had no dedicated landing craft at the time of Operation Barbarossa. As if the stops were pulled out, the combination of renewed military thinking and industrial might developed a considerable range of assets, producing a variety of different landing craft classes between 1942 and 1945.

Landing tenders were designed to fulfil a vital and important role for the besieged city of Leningrad (St Petersburg) in 1942. Built by the War Council of Leningrad Front to cross Lake Ladoga to the north-east of the city, the tenders helped to supply food, ammunition and troops as well as evacuate citizens. The design was simple and distinctly utilitarian in nature, with the hull made from several flat sheets of steel welded together.

They were built to three variants: Number 11 the one-hold version with a 12-ton capacity followed by the Number 16 build with two holds and capable of carrying 15 tons and the larger Number 19, again with two holds and a 25-ton capacity. Tenders 11 and 16 could transport 70 people whilst Number 19 could transport 90, with each craft manned by five crew.

All three craft had a shared high draft of 1.1m (3.6ft) with the Number 11 craft being 10.3m (33.8ft) long with a beam of 3.3m (10.8ft); Number 16 was 10.7m (35ft) long with a beam of 3.6m (11.8ft), whilst Number 19 was 14.4m (47.2ft) long with a beam of 3.8m (12.5ft). All three were powered by 73hp petrol engines. Craft 11 and 16 were capable of 6 knots whilst 19 could achieve 5 knots with an average of 80nm (148km or 88 miles) endurance.

Number 1 Landing Boat was a steel-hulled landing motorboat designed by Gorky Design Bureauand powered by two petrol automobile motors with 174hp. With a crew of three, this 14.6m- (47.9ft-) long and 3.6m- (11.8ft-) wide craft could transport up to 60 troops. Some would see service as minesweeping vessels later in the war.

The DB pr.165 Landing Boat or Desant Bot (DB) landing craft was designed in late 1941, like the Number 1 Landing Boat, with the Gorky Design Bureau ordered to plan an all-steel craft for amphibious operations. The bureau eventually came out with the 15.2m- (50ft-) long DB pr.165, which included an armoured coxswain's position; it was driven by two 85hp GAZ-202 petrol engines. As well as being capable of carrying up to 60 personnel, a light gun and vehicle could also be carried on a temporary deck covering the main cargo well.

As well as Lend-Lease US LCVs and LCTs, the Soviets also used a variety of captured German and Japanese craft.

Axis Landing Craft

Whilst the Western Allies were busy developing their craft and doctrine, so too were the Axis powers. Again, this was in part as a result of strategic and tactical necessity, especially in the case of the Imperial Japanese armed forces whose campaigns would mean crossing vast tracts of water.

For the Germans their greatest seaborne adventure would have been Operation Sea Lion. However, the Battle of Britain, a strong Royal Navy Home Fleet, lack of access to the necessary powered vessels, coupled with the approaching autumn storms, put paid to any ambitions on the part of the Kriegsmarine and Heer. That said, preparations were advanced enough for the gathering of nearly 2,500 barges and lighters, along with the development of a waterproofed Panzer III. This 'adapt what you have' attitude was prevalent throughout the German military, and landing craft were no exception. The preparation of the commandeered barges assembled from across Northern Europe was fairly well advanced by the time of cancellation by Hitler on 17 September 1940, though feint preparations continued into early October to keep the pressure on Britain.

However, it was the lack of specifically designed landing craft available for Sea Lion that highlighted to the German High Command of the Armed Forces (Oberkommando der Wehrmacht or OKW) the need for such craft. As a result, the first Naval Landing Craft, or Marinefährprahm (MFP – literally 'artillery ferry') was developed, first entering service in spring 1941. Designed for logistics work, these large craft were capable of transporting 200 personnel or 140 tons of

German MFPs were transferred to the Mediterranean to supplement Italian-built landing craft intended for the invasion of Malta. (Bundesarchiv)

equipment, including armour, as well as a complement of between 17 and 25 crew.

The steel hulls were fitted with a single bow ramp fitted to the front; the cargo well could be covered to protect contents from water damage. The MFP was powered by three Deutz truck engines, giving a combined power output of 390hp capable of propelling the MFP at 10.5 knots – a decent speed given that the hull was protected by 20mm-thick steel armour plating and 100mm concrete protection – which in turn gave the MFP a range of 421nm (779km or 463 miles).

As with Allied landing craft, the MFP hulls were easily adapted and were divided into a range of classes with varying uses, including the Artilleriefährprahm (AFP) hull which was fitted with two 88mm guns and light AA guns, as well as the Italian-built Motozattera. The MFP was used in almost all key operational areas such as the English Channel, the Mediterranean and the Black Sea.

A smaller naval supply lighter called Marine Nachschub Leichter or MNL was introduced into service in mid-1944 in the midst of the Allied advance into Northern Europe. The timing could not have been better in some respects as these lighter craft were able to operate on canals and rivers as logistics support and landing craft. The design was modular, featuring six 18-ton sections that were delivered by rail before being assembled, with a help of a crane, over a period of 48 hours. Whilst the MNL featured bow doors, it wasn't fitted with a ramp which slowed the loading and unloading process.

Powered by two diesel engines producing 240hp, the MNL had a top speed of 10 knots and a range of 540nm (999km or 594 miles). The MNL featured two weather-protected internal cargo holds with light vehicles and artillery carried on the deck. Loading was aided by a 2-ton boom track carrier. The MNL was 38m (125ft) long and 5m (16.5ft) in the beam. For protection from prowling aircraft, the MNL carried a 37mmm Flak gun mounted to the rear and a 20mm Flakvierling 38 on the bridge roof. The MNL carried a crew of between nine and 14 personnel.

The Marine Artillerieleichter (MAL) was a flat-bottomed craft specifically designed for Operation Barbarossa, being 35m (115ft) in length and 8.6m (28ft) in the beam. These had been intended to operate on the Caspian Sea. Powered by two Deutz diesels producing 260bhp, these gave the MAL a top speed of 8.5 knots and a range of 790nm (1,462km or 869 miles). The MALs, like the MNLs, were of modular design, with the ten sections following the advancing troops by rail and road before being constructed within a period of 48 hours.

Although capable of carrying two Panzer III/IVs, the MAL was not equipped with a ramp system; instead, like the MNL, it relied upon a loading track along which trolleys would be manually cranked. The MAL could also carry up to 200 troops, two heavy trucks or six standard trucks. For protection the MNAL could be fitted with a range of anti-aircraft guns including the formidable 20mm Flakvierling 38 quad gun. This meant the MAL was substantially manned with 21 crew and 29 personnel manning the various weapons.

The Siebelfähre or Siebel catamaran barge was perhaps the most versatile of the German solutions to transporting men and matériel across bodies of water, seeing use throughout the war. Developed for Sea Lion in 1940, the Siebelfähre was used in a range of theatres. The brainchild of Field Marshal Walther von Brauchitsch, Commander-in-Chief (Oberbefehlshaber) of the German Army and designed by aircraft engineer and Luftwaffe colonel Fritz Siebel, the first prototypes were built from salvaged Schwere Schiffsbrücke (heavy pontoons). These pontoons were then arranged as a catamaran connected by steel crossbeams.

This arrangement was ultimately powered by four Ford V8s generating 300hp capable of moving the craft at 11 knots and giving it a range of 300nm (555km or 330 miles); it crewed by between 11 and 14 personnel. The Siebelfähre was intended to carry transport and light artillery loads with a typical load being one 88mm gun and two 20mm guns with tractors. After the cancellation of Sea Lion, the Siebelfähre were shared among all three arms of the Wehrmacht where they saw service on inland waterways or fulfilling roles such as minelaying

The Pionierlandungsbooten (PilaBo) 39, 40 and 41 were developed as specialist tank landing craft designed by the Bodan Shipyard of Kressbronn on the shores of Lake Constance. The first Pionierlandungsbooten were deployed operationally in September 1940. For carriage, the 20-ton PilaBo 39 was split in two halves along the length of its 15m (49ft) hull, each side sitting comfortably on a standard railway platform wagon; once assembled, the PilaBo's beam sat at 4.7m (15.5ft) wide. The PilaBo 39 was propelled by two 86hp diesel engines, making for a top speed of 11 knots. It was capable of carrying a 200-ton load with ease.

The Pilabo 40 followed with the same engine layout and assembly in halves but with larger dimensions at 19m (62ft) long by 5.9m (19ft) wide. It weighed 30 tons and

Pionierlandungsboot 39 in Italian service. Note the camouflage patterning. (Bundesarchiv)

German Luftwaffe anti-aircraft Siebel ferry at Lahdenpohja, Finland. (Government of Finland)

was capable of carrying a load of 30 tons. Like the PilaBo 39, the 40 was manned by a crew of seven.

As with all things operational, experience led to an improved version, the PilaBo 41, built in 1942. This was fractionally larger than the 39 and 40 versions at 19.3m (63.4ft) long by 5.9m (19.3ft) wide at the beam. The PilaBo41 weighted 35 tons and was capable of carrying up to 40 tons. It was powered by two 120hp engines, which gave it a speed of up to 10.8 knots. The PilaBo 41 looked more like contemporary Allied craft as it was fitted with the familiar bow ramp. To the rear the crew of seven were treated to an enclosed wheelhouse.

The final in-service PilaBo was the 43, a shore-to-shore craft with a roll-on-roll-off capacity. The 43 was almost double the length of its predecessors at 35.5m (116.5ft) long by 8.6m (28ft) wide. Its total displacement was 145 tons and it was capable of carrying a 100-ton payload, or 230 troops. It was armed with a light Flak gun on its starboard side. Like the other PilaBos, the 43 was capable of being transported by rail, split into three separate modules for the journey.

There existed a range of smaller craft available too, with the design and development almost echoing that of the USMC experience. Initial designs were based on launches, much like the Higgins's Eureka tugboat and domestic designs such as the petrol-powered Pferdeboot or 'horse boat'. This craft was used to transport ten horses or 70 men in the First World War. With a draft of 0.6m (2ft) it could be used as a ship-to-shore lighter, or bank-to-bank ferry.

The most prolific of the German landing craft were the Infanterietransporter types, the I-O, I-A and the F.V.B 3. The I-O and I-A were reminiscent of the early Higgins LCP(L)s with troops exiting over the bows. Designed once again by Colonel Siebel, these craft were 18m (59ft) long and 4m (13ft) at the beam. The craft were powered by a mix of engines; the I-O used either two Ford (82hp), Opel (62hp) or Maybach (125hp) petrol engines or Daimler-Benz (125hp) diesels. The I-A used either the 200bhp BMW VIU petrol engine or 200hp Henschel diesels. These gave the I-O and the I-A an average speed of 10 knots, a

Quite possibly the last surviving example of a *Pionierlandungsboot* 41. Note wheelhouse and ramp arrangement. (Mosbatho)

capacity to carry 40 personnel or 7 tons of stores, with had a crew of eight.

The F.V.B 3, introduced in 1942, featured a bow ramp, and was 20m (65.6ft) long and 3.1m (10ft) wide at the beam. Like the I-O and I-A, the F.V.B 3 weighed 20 tons and was capable of carrying the same load. Powered by two petrol engines which produced 200hp, the F.V.B 3 was capable of running at 11.3 knots.

These were followed in 1943 by the diesel-powered 8-ton SchäLB 600, which could cruise at a mere 6 knots and was capable of transporting 5 tons of cargo, 40 men or one light truck and gun. Some 200 SchäLB 600s were produced. Its main area of service was in the fjords of Norway and as such it had quite a high draft for such a light craft: 0.9.m (3ft).

The Italian Navy, the Regia Marina, were also developing their landing craft force, especially keeping a weather-eye on the situation on the nearby islands of Malta and Gozo. In the autumn of 1941, the Regia Marina ordered the construction of 100 wooden landing craft known as Motolance (ML). This design was a big departure for the Italians as they continued to field barges for landing personnel that wouldn't have looked out of place at Gallipoli.

Each ML carried a crew of nine along with 30 troops in a design very similar to the LCP(L). The key difference was that the

ML featured a single tub for the carriage of troops, which kept their heads below the top of the hull. It also featured a small ramp and bow doors similar to the British LCA. The ML had a displacement of 15.5 tons and was 14m (46ft) in length. It was fitted with two diesel engines, which gave it a speed of 12 knots and was fitted with a single 13.2mm machine gun in the bow.

The larger Motozaterra (MZ) was the Italian version of the Marinefahrpram, this ship again intended to support the invasion of Malta, whilst becoming the first large landing craft in use with the Regia Marina. The MZ was able to carry three M13/40 medium tanks along with 100 infantrymen. They were powered by locally produced truck engines, 150hp six-cylinder OM BXDs, and protected by a 3in/40 QF Breda gun.

By mid-1942 the first batch of MZs were in service, and as a result of their work in covering the shore-to-shore route from Italy to Libya, the Regia Marina ordered a second batch of MZs which featured modifications including a raised bow and strengthened keel to improve seaworthiness. This second batch of MZs was fitted with larger fuel tanks to increase range as well as 100mm-thick concrete armour and a second Breda 20mm AA gun mounted amidships. In total 95 MZs were operated by the Regia Marina.

An Italian motorbike team landing at Sitia, Crete, on 27 May 1941. These types of experience led to the construction of the ML and later MZ fleet. (Unknown)

The Japanese, as previously mentioned, had led the way with the contemporary design with the bow-ramped Dai Hatsu-class landing craft. The Dai Hatsu was 14.6m (48ft) long, its hull was constructed from welded metal sheet, and it was powered by a diesel engine which gave it a speed of 8 knots. It weighed 10.5 tons and was capable of carrying 10 tons of stores, including wheeled vehicles. The Dai Hatsu saw service not only in the Second World War but also the Second Sino-Japanese War (1937–45). It could be modified to carry weapons of up to 37mm calibre as well as being fitted with appliqué armour, which was effective against gunfire from weapons of up to 40mm calibre. A much lighter wooden version, the Moku Hatsu, was produced as steel supplies diminished, at 15m (49ft) long and 3.6m (12ft) wide at the beam. It was mostly used for supply duties in calm waters.

A further development was the 17.6m- (58ft-) long and 3.7m- (12ft-) wide Toku Dai Hatsu-class landing craft which was capable of carrying either a Type 97 Chi-Ha medium-sized tank or two eight-ton Type 95 Ha-Go light tanks. This all-metal craft was remarkable in having quite a shallow draft of only 0.9m (3ft) and was powered by a 150hp diesel engine which gave it a speed of 9 knots.

The final craft of the class was the 4.4-ton Sho Hatsu which was the smallest of the Hatsu class of landing craft. It omitted

US landing on Attu Island, 11 May 1943, using captured Dai Hatsu landing craft, hence the large flag. (USN)

a ramp for a single bow and was used for the carriage of stores from ship to shore. A mere 10.6m (35ft) long and 2.44m (8ft) in width, the Sho Hatsu had a draft of 0.6m (2ft) and was capable of carrying 4 tons of stores. Powered by 60hp kerosene engine, the Sho Hatsu could cruise at steady speed of 7 knots.

Amphibians

As landing craft continued to proliferate, so too did the challenges. In continental Europe canals, rivers and swamps were often simply unsuitable for crossing with a landing craft. Whilst smaller craft were available for bank-to-bank river crossings, these were often unsuitable, dangerous and slow, and advancing forces often needed something a more robust. In the Pacific theatre the coral reefs presented their own challenges to operational planners, sailors and attacking troops.

The designers got to work to overcome these issues and the solution that all parties came up with was the design and use of specialist amphibious vehicles. The two key Allied tracked amphibious vehicles were the Landing Vehicle, Tracked (LVT), and the M29 Weasel and M29C Water Weasel. There were also wheeled amphibians which included the near-legendary DUKW, which would spawn the Soviet BAV485, a reverse-engineered copy, the Ford GPA and the Thornycroft Terrapin.

The LVT was initially designed in 1935 as a swamp rescue vehicle, known as the *Alligator* by the designer and inventor Donald Roebling. The LVT family soon included troop-carrier and fire-support versions. The USMC learned of the *Alligator* from a *Life* magazine article, and approached Roebling to design a version that was more tailored to military use in a ship-to-shore environment.

Initially Roebling was reluctant to get involved as he saw only peaceful civilian applications for his *Alligator,* whilst the USN felt the role it would fulfil was already catered for with its growing landing craft fleet. However, with the advent of war, Roebling relented and in May 1940 the first military prototype appeared. At this point the USN's Bureau of Ships got involved and requested a second prototype, this time equipped with a more powerful engine. It was this design that the USMC tested in November 1940 with positive results, which led to the Bureau of Ships placing an initial contract for 100 units of a more rugged and more easily assembled all-steel model. The first LVT-1, as the new model was known, was delivered in July 1941. Interestingly a further 200 units were ordered even before the first-production units were delivered – these were made by Food Machinery Corporation (FMC). FMC would draw on their LVT production experience to produce the famous post-war M113 Armoured Personal Carrier.

LVT crews assemble along a shoreline to undergo training on the M2. (USN)

An LVT with a 37mm being put through its paces cross-country. (NARA)

The first LVT was capable of carrying 24 troops or 2,000kg (4,500lb) of cargo. Although lacking in armour and ruggedness on hard surfaces, the USMC knew the LVT would develop into a fine vehicle. Indeed, their use in the Guadalcanal campaign proved their worth as they ferried stores from ship to shore throughout the operation.

The LVT-1 was powered by a 146hp six-cylinder petrol engine, which was housed in the rear cargo hold and gave the LVT a speed of 6 knots in the water and 12mph (19km/h) on land. The LVT-1 was fitted with Roebling-patented oblique shoes designed to give excellent grip on swamp land and sand, propelling the LVT through water. The LVT had a range of 210 miles (340km) on land or 60 miles (100km) in water. Apart from the forward driver's compartment, the steel hull was designed to carry cargo in several watertight compartments. For supporting and defensive fire, the LVT-1 could be fitted with two .30 M1919 Browning machine guns.

User feedback and experiences from first combat use led to the initial design being refined, though the new model's development was sluggish as a result of it becoming a complete redesign. This new model would be known as the LVT-2 Buffalo.

Although Roebling had initially been reluctant to produce a vehicle for the military, he had drafted a turreted support version in 1940. This design languished until summer 1941 when the USMC recommended development of an LVT with a 37mm main gun and three machine guns; this model was also expected to be armoured against hits from .50- (12.7mm-) calibre rounds.

The new fire support versions were fitted with turrets from the Stuart M3 family of light tanks and became known as Amtanks (LVT(A)-1). These appeared alongside Howitzer Motor Carriage M8-turreted versions known as LVT(A)-4s. Other developments included a new powerpack and cooling system, also from the Stuart family, as well as a new rubber 'torsilastic' suspension which improved the LVT's land performance. Such was the LVT's success that the Secretary of the Navy formed the Continued Board for the Development of the Landing Vehicle Tracked on 30 October 1943. This meant that production continued throughout the war, with in 18,616 LVTs delivered.

The M29 in its usual guise. This loaded example belongs to Charlie Company, 121st Engineer Combat Battalion (ECB), 29th US Infantry Division. (NARA)

DUKWs of 56 Water Transport Unit, Royal Army Service Corps (RASC), loaded with Japanese ammunition collected from dumps in Singapore. The ammunition will be transferred to landing craft before being dumped at sea. (IWM)

The M29 Weasel was initially designed as an air-droppable, lightweight, 1,700kg (3,800lb) tracked personnel carrier. It was envisaged that it would assist commandos in crossing areas of snow to attack sites of scientific importance, such as heavy water plants, in Norway. Part of its in-service development saw the arrival of the M29C Water Weasel, which whilst not as rugged as the LVT series, preformed its duties mostly on inland waterways and close to shore as a result of its low freeboard (the distance between its upper edge of the hull and surface of the water). Fitted with buoyancy cells in the bow and stern as well as twin rudders, the M29C had a suitably shaped hull. The M29C could only operate in inland waterway conditions, so its shoreline use was limited though it did see action in the Pacific theatre, most notably at Okinawa.

Build by car giant Studebaker, the M29 was fitted with .5m (20in) rubber tracks and powered by a Studebaker Model 6-170 Champion 70hp engine fitted at the front, and operating a rear-wheel-drive system. This gave the M29C a maximum speed of 36mph (58km/h) on land and a range of 168 miles (266km).

The General Motors Company (GMC) *D* (Designed in 1942), *U* (Utility), *K* (All-wheel drive), *W* (Dual rear axles) DUKW (BAV485) is synonymous with Second World War amphibian vehicles, from the Pacific to Northern Europe. A shore-to-shore vehicle capable of carrying 24 troops or 2,300kg (5,000lb) of stores, the DUKW was as remarkable looking as it was remarkable as an amphibious asset. Through the use of a special frame, the DUKW could be coupled with another DUKW to help ferry bulkier stores, including aircraft.

The DUKW was designed by naval architects Rod Stephens Jr. of yacht designers Sparkman & Stephens, Inc. and Briton Dennis Puleston, also a deep-water sailor, and Frank W. Speir from the Massachusetts Institute of Technology. The three designed the DUKW under the auspices of the National Defense Research Committee and the Office of Scientific Research and Development to solve the problem of resupply to units which had just performed an amphibious landing.

The DUKW was very nearly rejected for service, but saved as a result of a dramatic event that occurred during the trial of an experimental vehicle near Provincetown, Massachusetts. A US Coast Guard craft had run aground on a sandbar during a storm. With 69mph winds, rain and heavy surf preventing rescue teams getting to the stranded craft and its crew of seven, the DUKW had no issues, and tore through the surf, rescuing the stranded Coast Guards. This secured its future.

The DUKW was built around the chassis of the GMC AFKWX, a cab-over-engine (COE) version of GMC's ubiquitous CCKW six-wheel-drive truck, which had been surrounded with a shaped watertight hull, along with propeller and rudder. It was powered by a 91hp GMC Model 270 straight-six engine coupled to a five-speed overdrive transmission. This in turn would drive a transfer case for the propeller, and a two-speed transfer case to the axles. The propeller and front axle were selectable from their own transfer case. A power take-off was also included on the transmission which drove an air-compressor and rear-mounted winch. The DUKW could also mount a .50-calibre machine gun on a ring mount.

The DUKW weighed 6,200kg (13,600lb) empty and had a top speed of 50mph (80km/h) on road and 5.5 knots on the water. It was 9.5m (31ft) long, 2.5m (8ft 3 in) wide, 2.18m (7ft 2in) high with the folding-canvas top stowed and 2.6m (8ft 9in) high with the top up. As the DUKW was only fitted with sheet steel between 1.6 and 3.2mm (1/16 and 1/8 inch) thick to help minimize weight, it was supplied with a high-capacity bilge pump system to keep the DUKW afloat should the hull be breached with holes up to 2in (51mm) in diameter.

The DUKW was the first vehicle to give the driver control over the tyre pressure from inside the cab. This allowed the tyres to be fully inflated for hard surfaces such as roads or deflated for softer surfaces, such as beach sand. This feature is now standard on many military vehicles including the AM General Humvee high-mobility truck. By the time production had ended in 1945, 21,147 DUKWs had been manufactured.

The Ford GPA, or Seep, modelled on the highly successfully Jeep, sadly lacked the ingredients to make it an equal success, dogged by heavy land handling and poor water performance. The GPA had its genesis in a directive from the National Defense Research Committee (NDRC) for the design of a vehicle to be designated the QMC-4 ¼-Ton Truck Light Amphibian.

Once again, naval architect Roderick Stephens Jr. was asked to design the hull for a 1,200kg (2,700lb) amphibious jeep, using the same approach as his design for the DUKW. Like the DUKW, the Seep was fitted with a power take-off-driven screw propeller, placed in a dedicated tunnel fairing in the stern along with the rudder. The construction of the vehicle was developed by armoured-car maker and all-wheel-drive specialists Marmon-Herrington, and Ford. The Marmon-Herrington prototype used a welded sheet-metal hull formed around an integral structure. Ford used a sturdy chassis and internal frame to which they welded

A casualty being loaded into a DUKW on the beach at Fossacesia, Italy. Note the camouflage finish and the rope fenders. (IWM)

A Ford GPA making a splash during training at Camp Carson, Colorado. The Ford GPA failed to deliver and many found themselves on the Eastern Front supporting Soviet advances. (NARA)

This restored Seep sits handsomely in front of its German counterpart, the Type 166 Schwimmwagen. (Alf van Beem)

standard automotive sheet-steel. This approach made the GPA 180kg (40lb) lighter than the Marmon-Herrington prototype.

It had a further edge in that it used as many elements of the standard Jeeps as possible which would save money and simplify logistical considerations. The interior was similar to the Jeep's, though due to the nature of the vehicle, the driver was in command of a few more switches and levers. These included drive controls, the bow-mounted capstan winch control, propeller deployment and rudder control. After a direct comparison of the two prototypes, Ford was awarded the contract for the GPA in 1942.

In contrast to the DUKW, the GPA did not perform well in the field. At some 1,600kg (3,500lb) the production truck had become much heavier than the original 1,200kg (2,600lb) specified in the design brief, but its volume had not been increased accordingly. As a consequence, a low freeboard meant that the GPA could not handle more than a light chop or carry much cargo. The GPA's intended use of ferrying troops and cargo from ships offshore, over a beach and continuing inland, was therefore very limited.

On land, the GPA proved to be unpopular with the troops due to its poor handling, and ironically, they would often flounder in shallow water, which, rather embarrassingly, the regular Jeep could ford with ease. As a result of operational feedback, production was halted in March 1943, and most GPAs were sent to the Soviet Union under the Lend-Lease programme, which were later reverse-engineered as the GAZ-46 MAV, where they excelled in the reconnaissance role.

A Terrapin awaits its next tasking during the Battle of the Scheldt, 13 October 1944, whilst the DUKWs move forward. (National Archives of Canada)

Light amphibious tank T-38 keeps sentinel outside the Kubinka Tank Museum, Russia. (Alf van Beem)

The British Thornycroft Terrapin came about as a result of the shortage of US-manufactured DUKWs. Heavy vehicle manufacturer Thornycroft was commissioned by the Ministry of Supply to design an amphibious vehicle capable filling the gap in the motor pool that the DUKW would have filled, with the same role, to ferry supplies and troops from ship to shore.

The Terrapin was powered by two centrally mounted side-by-side Ford V8 engines, which produced 190hp, each motor driving the wheels on either side of the vehicle with directional control achieved by wheel braking. The danger here was that should an engine fail, the whole vehicle would swing violently. The two engine bays split the cargo bay in two restricting the size and type of load that could be carried, which could be up to 4 tons.

The 8x8 Terrapin used its four middle wheels to travel on a level surface, whilst the raised fore and aft wheels provided traction on slippery surfaces such as riverbanks. When used in the water, the Terrapin was moved by two rear-mounted propellers. Due to the large-diameter tyres, the Terrapin was a relatively high vehicle at 2.92m (9ft 7in) and, even though it was open-topped, it was difficult to enter and exit.

Given the height of the vehicle, the driver was hampered by poor visibility due to his central position within the vehicle. This poor view was hampered further when the forward cargo bay's canvas cover was used. In this situation the driver had to be guided by another member of the crew who could see the route ahead.

The Terrapin was, like its namesake, rather slow, and not suited to rough seas, due mostly to its restricted length of 7m (23ft) versus the DUKW's 9.4m (31ft). These issues led to the development of a Mark 2 which owed much more in appearance to the DUKW, though this was soon abandoned as availability of DUKWs improved. Some 500 Terrapins were built by Morris Commercial.

The Soviets had placed the focus of their amphibious deigns around the chassis of light tanks. The first of these, the T-37A, was based on the Vickers-Carden-Loyd light amphibious tank, which had not been taken into British service but did become a sales success for Vickers. Whilst a sound idea, and one that made sense given the proliferation of waterways in Russia alone, in practice, the T37A was a great idea but was less than successful. Its limited range, coupled with poor buoyancy and transmission issues, as well as its tendency to slip tracks whilst moving, did not endear it to its crews.

Engineers under Chief Designer N. Astrov and Chief Engineer N. Kozyrev of Factory Number 37 set to improving the T-37A. However, the extent of the redesign was such that the project became the T-38. The prototype was completed by June 1935 and the new T-38 retained many of the features of the T-37A. This included its 40hp GAZ engine and hand-operated turret, which was moved to the left-hand side of the vehicle as well as switching the positions of the two-man crew.

The T-38 was also slightly wider at 3.3m (11ft) versus the T-37A's 2.1m (7ft) and lower at 1.6m (5ft 2in) versus 1.8m (5ft 9in), giving it additional buoyancy that made the cork buoys used on the T-37A redundant. The production T-38 was armed with a 7.62mm DT machine gun, as the prototype's 20mm ShVAK cannon impaired the driver's ability to control the tank.

The T-38 was primarily designed for reconnaissance and infantry support roles, taking advantage of its low silhouette and improved ground and water mobility. The T-38 was also intended to be air-portable and could be carried under the fuselage of a Tupolev TB-3 bomber. As a light amphibian it lacked armour, firepower and in most cases a radio, severely limiting its use. It was able to carry two soldiers whilst making water crossings, though anything weighing more than 120kg (264lb) would see water enter the vehicle via the commander's hatch. By 1941 these flaws, combined with experience from the First Soviet-Finnish War, led to the T-38 slowly falling out of favour and being relegated to support roles, including artillery tractor.

These flaws were fixed by the T-40 amphibious scout. The coil-spring suspension of the T-38 was replaced by a torsion-bar suspension coupled to four pairs of road wheels. Unlike the riveted hulls of the T-37 and T-38, the T-40 was constructed with a boat-shaped welded hull which was topped by a welded, conical turret. The turret housed a single yet formidable 12.7mm DShK heavy machine gun, although overall the armour remained thin. The T-40 also saw the amphibian tank grow in length, from the 3.8m (12ft 4in) T-37A/T-38 to 4.1m (13.5ft). The T-40 was also fitted with a propeller recessed into the rear hull, which also offered protection to the propeller.

Only a small number of T-40s were built before the German invasion, which left both the T-37A and T-38 to remain in service and form the bulk of the Red Army's amphibious tank force. Despite all this hard work during the Second World War, the main amphibious scout vehicle of the Red Army would become the Lend-Lease Ford GPAs.

The Type 166 Schwimmwagen was an amphibious development of the famous Kübelwagen used by all branches of the Wehrmacht during the war. Its engine and mechanics came from the Type 86 four-wheel-drive prototype of the Kübelwagen and the Type 87 four-wheel-drive 'Kübel/Beetle' command vehicle. Designed by Posrche's lead designer Erwin Komenda, the Schwimmwagen utilized a new body tub structure to enable smooth passage though water.

Taking the salute. A Type 166 Schwimmwagen with unidentified general staff, passes a group of officers. (Bundesarchiv)

Under new management: men of 23rd Hussars add their markings to a captured Schwimmwagen, July 1944. (IWM)

The early prototypes, known as Type 128s, were based on the Kübelwagen's 2.4m (7ft 10in) wheelbase fitted with a custom-welded body tub. This approach demonstrated that this construction method was too weak for offroad use due to a lack of rigidity, as well as hull ruptures at the front cross-member and wheel wells. To avoid these obvious flaws in an amphibious vehicle, the Type 166 models, which rolled off the production lines in 1941, were smaller with a reduced wheel base of 2.0m (6ft 7in), the overall length being 3.8m (12ft 7in), with a width of 1.5m (4ft 10in) and with a relatively low silhouette of 1.6m (5ft 4 in).

The output from Volkswagen and Porsche of the Type 166 was prodigious. With production running until 1944 the Schwimmwagen became the most produced amphibious car in history, with a total of 15,584 units built.

Designed by Rheinmetall-Borsig the 13-ton, 8.6m (28ft 3in) long and 3.16m (10ft 4in) wide Landwasserschelpper (LWS) was intended to be used as an waterways

Right: Landwasserschlepper (LWS) in early field grey finish on the move showing its distinctive boat-shaped design. (Unknown)

Below: A Type 2 Ka-Mi Amphibious Tank comes ashore during trials carried out by 2/4 Armoured Regiment (Australia) in Talili Bay, Rabaul, New Britain. (AWM)

engineering support vehicle. Ordered in 1935 by the Heereswaffenamt, the German Army Weapons Agency, the LWS was intended to act as a lightweight waterways tug with some capacity to operate on land. The hull of the LWS was similar to that of a motor launch controlled by rear-mounted tunnelled propellers and twin rudders. On to the lower hull tracks were added for land passage.

The Landwasserschlepper was first demonstrated to General Franz Halder, Chief of Staff of the Army High Command (OKH), on 2 August 1940 by the Reinhardt trials staff on the island of Sylt. Halder was critical of the LWS's high silhouette of 3.1m (10ft 3in) when out of the water, though he could see that the design benefits outweighed this particular sticking point.

By the autumn of 1940, three prototypes were assigned to Tank Detachment 100 as part of Operation Sea Lion with the intention of utilizing the LWSs to pull ashore the many unpowered assault barges that would be used during the invasion, as well as being used as general towing and recovery vehicles. As a secondary task the LWS would also carry supplies ashore whilst the barges were grounded. This involved the use of a specifically designed trailer, known as the Kässbohrer amphibious trailer, which was capable of transporting 10–20 tons of freight. The plan was to produce enough LWS units so give each invasion barge access to at least one LWS. However, difficulties in the mass-production process of the LWS prevented this occurring.

Due to its somewhat prolonged development, the LWS only entered service in limited numbers until 1942 where it was used on the Eastern Front and in the North Africa campaign. Although a second version, the LWSII, based on the chassis of a Panzer IV, was trialled, it was not adopted, thus leaving the LWS in use until the end of the war in 1945.

Given their geographical location, the Imperial Japanese Army (IJA) developed a range of amphibious vehicles for military use, experimenting extensively throughout the late 1920s and early 1930s. By 1940 the Imperial Japanese Navy (IJN) had taken the lead in developing amphibious assets, and worked with Mitsubishi to develop the earlier IJA ideas.

The first vehicle was a tracked Type 1 Mi-Sha which was used in the development of the Type 2 Ka-Mi which was produced in 1942. The 12-ton (9.15 tons without pontoons) Type 2 Ka-Mi was designed for IJN naval infantry units of the Special Naval Landing Forces (SNLF), to land at locations without port facilities as part of an amphibious tank unit, as well as being used for special operations. It carried a high-velocity Type 1 37mm main gun, along with a coaxial 7.7mm Type 97 light machine gun with a second Type 97 located in the tank's bow. The tank was capable

Type 2 Ka-Mi tanks on board a 2nd class transporter of the Imperial Japanese Navy. Note the hull floatation attachment points. (IJN)

of making 5 knots in the water and had a range of 140km (87 miles); it was driven by two propellers situated at the rear of the hull, powered by the tank's engine. The commander controlled the rudders from the turret via cables. The five-man crew also included an onboard mechanic.

The Type 2 was based on the army's Type 95 Ha-Go light tank, but replaced the rivetted hull with an all-welded type complete with rubber seals to ensure it was watertight. For extra buoyancy large steel-plate pontoons were attached to the glacis plate and rear decking. The front pontoon was internally divided into two sections, with each further divided into three separate watertight compartments to minimize any negative effects of battle damage on the pontoon's integrity. The pontoons were secured to the Type 2 by clips that could be released from the interior of the tank once a landing had been made. The pontoons affected Type 2's size, making it 7.4m long (24ft), 4.8m (15ft 7in) without flotation pontoons), 2.8m (9ft 1in) wide and 2.3m (7ft 5in) high.

The Type 2 came into active service after the initial IJN/IJA campaigns of the Second World War, missing the operations for which it was initially designed. Nonetheless the Type 2 went on to be used successfully in a range of operations including Guadalcanal, Saipan and Leyte.

On the heels of the Type 2 design came the larger more powerfully armed Type 3 Ka-Chi, with the prototype completed in late 1943 and the first units entering service soon after. Known as the Special Type 3 Launch Ka-Chi, the Type 3 was considered to be a medium tank, modified from the Type 2 to include two extra road wheels and two more return rollers on either side of its body. This gave the Type 3 a length of 10.3m (34ft) with pontoons, a width of 3m (9ft 8in) and a height of 3.8m (12ft 5in), with an overall weight of 29 tons.

The Type 3 featured smooth sides that faired into the sheet-metal front and rear flotation pontoons. Like the Type 2, the front pontoon was shaped and both pontoons could be released from inside the tank once the landing had been made. However, the pontoons were rarely released by the crew as they afforded the tank additional protection against incoming fire. Again, like the Type 2, the Type 3's hull was welded and waterproofed with rubber seals. Propulsion came from twin screws, directed by two rudders. Behind the turret was a large snorkel for aerating the diesel engine more efficiently and prevent exhaust water ingress.

The Type 3 was armed with a Type 1 47mm main gun and a coaxial 7.7mm Type 97 machine gun, with a further Type 97 mounted in the hull. The vehicle had a crew of seven, including an onboard mechanic. Only 19 Type 3 Ka-Chis were built, from 1943 to 1945, but it was a useful piece of equipment that could to be launched from a submarine, to facilitate reinforcement of isolated island garrisons.

Another amphibian in IJA service was the 6.9m- (23ft-) long, 2.8m- (9ft-) wide F B military transport/personnel carrier used for crossing difficult, swampy terrain. First produced in 1935, the F B was crewed by up to three personnel. The F B featured eight road wheels either side, with rubber floats attached to the track links to help spread the weight of the 4.5-ton vehicle on soft ground. The F B was also capable of moving through water, powered by a propeller. A total of 146 F B units were built, along with a smaller 1.8-ton version known as the T B swamp scout vehicle. Sadly, no other details are available.

Post-War Developments

The post-war world of seaborne and amphibious operations was shaped by two equally important military events at the close of the Second World War: the advent of nuclear weapons and the helicopter. The proliferation of both would provide global challenges at strategic, tactical and political levels. These changes and challenges would have a great impact on the use and development of landing craft and amphibians.

Overall concepts remained very similar globally with traditional landing craft, such as the Landing Craft, Utility- (LCU-), and LCVP-based craft becoming the generic landing craft platforms. However, new technologies continued to evolve, the pinnacle of which was Sir Christopher Cockerell's refined hovercraft design, Landing Craft, Air Cushion (LCAC). This in turn would see the advent of a new form of support vessel, the giant Amphibious Assault Ships (AASs).

Whilst the West developed their seaborne long-reach options, the Soviets finally appeared to wake up. Perhaps enthused by Lend-Lease equipment and having the opportunity to study Allied doctrine, they also had the time to consider the practical applications of landing craft; the various design bureaus began to hone their techniques.

One key development was the Mexeflote is a molecular landing raft system, crewed by six personnel and capable of travelling in waves of up to 1.5m (4ft 11in) high. Powered by two Hydromaster six-cylinder diesels at 75hp each or two Thrustmaster OD150N propulsion units with a combined output of 150hp, the Mexeflote can provide the user with craft of three varying sizes. The standard is 20.1m (66ft) long with a beam of 7.4m (24ft) and capable of carrying

Below: Although a twenty-first-century photograph, this Royal Navy Landing Craft, Utility (LCU) has been in use since the late twentieth century. Note the camouflage scheme. (USN)

Bottom: New ways of working – an LCAC approaching the well deck of the Amphibious Assault Ship (AAS) USS *Wasp* during training off the coast of Camp Lejeune, NC, on 8 October 1997. (USN)

52 (Port) Squadron from 17 Port and Maritime Regiment deploying a Mexeflote. (Cpl Jamie Peters/RLC/MOD)

60,000kg (130,000lb). The maxi comes in two sizes; although the length, 38.4m (126ft), remains the same, the beam differs between 7.3m (24ft), which can carry 120,000kg (260,000lb) of stores and 12.2m (40ft) which carries 180,000kg (400,000lb) of stores. The Rhino would see action supporting Operation Corporate in the Falklands in 1982.

The Landing Craft, Utility (LCU) was the product of simplifications, taking the role of larger landing craft that emerged during the Second World War, and melding them into one affordable and more flexible platform. Numerous types were used in the mid- to late twentieth century by navies all over the globe, with many nations developing the larger LCTs and LCSs, using what they felt were the key elements of these craft to build craft that met their own needs. Some navies continued to use LCVPs for operations where troop numbers and equipment weights were lighter and where the tactical requirement demanded a smaller craft.

Meanwhile, the Landing Craft, Air Cushion (LCAC) was a quantum step forward with amphibious warfare utilizing the latest hovercraft technology. LCAC are often referred to as 'over the beach' (OTB) craft, an aspect of their character that gives them access to more than 70 per cent of the world's coastline, compared to a mere 15 per cent of coastline available to hulled landing craft. The LCAC's air cushion allows it to pass over soft sand, marsh and fenland as well as swampland and other loose coastal and inland surfaces at speeds often not matched by wheeled or tracked amphibians in similar circumstances. Like conventional landing craft, LCACs are often equipped with a range of mounted support weapons from light machines guns to surface-to-air missiles.

Understandably, the British were the first to realize the military benefits of the LCAC, and a series of trials took place between the Saunders Roe SR.N6, the British Hovercraft Corporation BH.7 and the Vosper Thorneycroft VT2. All three were exhaustively trialled by Naval Hovercraft Trials Unit, the Interservice Hovercraft Working Party and the Interservice Hovercraft (Trials) Unit (IHTU) at HMS *Ariel* (later HMS *Daedalus*), at Lee-on-the-Solent, west of Portsmouth harbour between 1961 and 1982. It would take a further decade until the Royal Marines received their first hovercraft, the Griffon Hoverwork (GHL) 2000TDX. The 2000TDX was known as the Landing Craft Air Cushion (Light) (LCAC(L)) in service. Measuring 12.7m (41ft 8in) in length with a beam of 6.1m (20ft), it is able to reach a speed in the water of 45 knots (8km/h or 52mph) and 30 knots (56km/h or 35mph) on land. The 2000TDX has a range in excess of 450 nautical miles (830km or 515

An LCVP, assigned to the surveying ship USNS *Chauvenet*, brings supplies ashore to a navigational aid site, 1981. (NARA)

The 2000TDX is a LCAC(L) currently in service with the Royal Marines. MoD

LCAC-55, a US Navy Landing Craft Air Cushion (LCAC), manoeuvres to enter the well deck of the amphibious assault ship USS *Kearsarge*. (USN)

miles) and is capable of transporting two crew and 16 marines.

The United States, with its understandably large littoral force, was keen to develop the concept of the LCAC. The first designs began in the early 1970s with the Amphibious Assault Landing Craft (AALC) test vehicle; in the following development stage, two further prototypes were built, JEFF A and JEFF B. JEFF A, which was later scuttled by the USN as part of Florida's artificial reef programme, was designed and built by Aerojet General in California. It featured four rotating ducted propellers, two fore and two aft.

A Soviet PT-76 light amphibious tank moves down the ramp of an 'Aist'-class air cushion vehicle. (NARA)

No more the warrior. This 'Gus'-class LCAC now sits as a museum piece at Severnoye Park, Tushino in Moscow. (Alan Wilson)

JEFF B was designed and built by Bell Aerospace in New Orleans, Louisiana, with two aft-mounted ducted propellers similar to the proposed SK-10 which was derived from the previous Bell SK-5/SR.N5 hovercraft that had been tested in Vietnam. The two craft confirmed the technical feasibility and operational capability that ultimately led to the JEFF B design being selected as the wining design basis for the LCAC. On 29 June 1987, LCAC was granted approval for full production with 48 craft authorized for purchase.

LCACs are transported in and operate from the US Navy's amphibious well decks of Amphibious Assault Ships (AAS). The LCAC operates with a crew of five. Apart from beach landings and all that these entail, it can also be used for evacuation support, lane breaching, mine countermeasure operations, as well as marine and special warfare equipment delivery. The four gas turbine engines are all used for lift and main propulsion, though the LCAC can operate on two engines should the need arise. The design of the LCAC allows it to operate in either a shore-to-shore or ship-to-shore role from as far as 50 nautical miles (93km or 58 miles) from the shoreline.

The LCAC is capable of carrying a 60-ton payload (up to 75 tons in an overload condition), including one M-1 Abrams tank, at speeds over 40 knots; it can also seat 180 troops. Exit is either via the bow ramp of 8.8m (28.8ft) width or the stern of 4.6m (15ft) width. The LCAC's overall length is

Left: A new-looking 'Kalmar' class LCAC on a transporter ship. (US DoD)

Below: A grounded 'Zubr'-class LCAC showing off her mass at a demonstration. (PH2 (AC) Mark Kettenhoffen, USN)

26.4m (87ft 11in) and its beam is 14.3m (47ft).

The Warsaw Pact, and post-Soviet/ Warsaw Pact states, also used a series of LCACs as did the Chinese People's Liberation Army Navy in a variety of guises and roles, much the same as NATO nations.

Type 722 Prototype 452 at rest at the Chinese Navy Museum, Qingdao, China. (Xeon)

Post-war Amphibians

All nations continued to develop the amphibian concept; for many it was a win-win, multipurpose platform, often able to fulfil a shore-to-shore role, cheap and easy to produce as well as being exceptionally flexible at a tactical level. Whilst the use of helicopters has almost eradicated the need for assault-type landing craft, the boom of amphibian development delivered an almost bewildering range of assets most notably among NATO and Warsaw Pact members. The amphibians listed below represent the most common types and is not intended to provide an exhaustive list, which would go well beyond the scope of this book.

Alvis Stalwart FV620/FV622/ FV623/ FV624

The Alvis Stalwart or Truck, High Mobility Load Carrier (HMLC), 5 ton, 6x6 was designed and built by British carmaker Alvis between 1963 and 1971 and was in service between 1964 and 1993. During this time, the Stalwart, based on the proven 6x6 chassis of the Saladin armoured car, served predominantly with the British Army of the Rhine (BAOR), providing logistical support. Capable of carrying 5 tons and towing 10 tons, the Stalwart was driven through the water at 6 knots by vectored thrust water-jet propulsion units.

Landing Vehicle, Tracked, Personnel-7 (LVTP-7)

The LVTP-7 was designed to replace the LVTP-5, improving unit reliability and vital vehicle systems, including replacing some vulnerable hydraulic systems with electric ones. The LVTP-7 also saw the introduction of two rear-mounted water jets to help give the LVTP-7 a top speed of 7 knots.

GAZ BTR 60/70/80

The BTR family of wheeled and tracked vehicles is synonymous with Soviet APCs. The eight-wheeled BTR 60/70/80 series fielded by all Warsaw Pact nations as well as numerous overseas states is instantly recognizable. Powered through the water by hydro jets, the BTR 80 is capable of speeds of over 5 knots. In Soviet use the BTR wheeled APCs were often used in a ship-to-shore role.

BMP Family

The BMP infantry fighting vehicles (IFV) first began making an appearance in the late 1960s and equipped several branches

of the Soviet armed forces, including the Marines. The BMP is propelled through water by its tracks, giving it a speed of 4 knots. A lightweight version the BMD series was produced for airborne use.

BMP Family

The BMP infantry fighting vehicles (IFV) first began making an appearance in the late 1960s and equipped several branches of the Soviet armed forces, including the Marines. The BMP is propelled through water by its tracks, giving it a speed of 4 knots. A lightweight version, the BMD series, was produced for airborne use.

An LVTP7 approaches Onslow Beach, North Carolina, during the field training Exercise Solid Shield '87. (DPLA)

A BMP making decent headway in calm waters. (Vitaly V. Kuzmin)

Landing Craft Variants

Landing craft, by their very nature, are variations on a theme, so most eventualities were catered for by bespoke craft such as the Landing Craft, Tank and the Landing Craft, Vehicle, Personnel. There were a range of variants and options available to commanders, and these grew as technology developed and operational requirements changed.

Landing Craft Tank (Rocket) (LCT(R))

The Landing Craft Tank (Rocket) (LCT(R)), was a modified LCT which carried 1,066 launchers for the British RP-3 60lb rocket, a weapon often carried by ground-attack aircraft such as the Hawker Typhoon, on its covered tank deck. The LCT(R) was a truly formidable asset which carried between 1,000 and 5,000 reloads, which gave the LCT a firepower equivalence of 200 destroyers. During operations the LCT(R) would anchor off the target beach, where rangefinding was achieved via a Type 970 radar set, form this the elevation of the launchers could be set accordingly. During firing the 17-man crew would retreat below whilst the commanding officer set off the launchers electrically from a special station. The launch could be controlled to provide an entire craft launch set or individual ranks of rockets.

Landing Craft Flak (LCF)

Landing Craft Flak (LCF) were converted LCTs designed to provide anti-aircraft support to any seaborne operation. The LCT's ramp was welded shut, with a deck built on top of the tank deck. The LCFs were equipped with several light anti-aircraft guns, with a typical fitting being eight 20mm Oerlikons and four QF 2-pounder pom-poms. British LCFs carried a crew of 60 including two naval officers and two Marine officers; the operation of the craft was the responsibility of the navy and the guns were manned by Royal Marines.

Landing Craft Gun (LCG)

The Landing Craft Gun (LCG) was another LCT conversion designed to provide supporting fire to landing forces and which came in three variants. As well as having the standard Oerlikon armament of a normal LCT, the LCG (Medium) weighted 250 tons and carried two 25-pounder gun-howitzers in armoured mountings, while LCG(L)3 and LCG(L)4 both weighed 500 tons and carried two 4.7in naval guns. The crewing of the LCG was similar to the LCF.

Landing Craft Support

There were several versions of the original Landing Craft Support (Medium) (LCS(M)). The Mark 2 and Mark 3 were operated by the Royal Navy and Royal Marines and were each armed with two .5in Vickers machine guns and a 4in mortar to fire smoke shells. The Fairmile H Landing Craft Support (Large) had additional armour added to its wooden hull and an anti-tank gun-mounted turret fitted. The LCS(L) Mk 1 had a Daimler armoured car turret fitted with a QF 2-pounder (40mm) gun whilst the Mk 2 carried the QF 6-pounder (57mm) anti–tank gun. USN Landing Craft Support were larger and were armed with a 3in gun, as well as various smaller-calibre weapons, as well as ten Mk 7 rocket launchers.

Left: Landing Craft Flak showing off its firepower. (IWM)

Below: Royal Marines in fighting mood man an LCS(M). These little craft were often used in the counter-submarine and -motorboat role.

Landing Craft in Detail

The range of landing craft and amphibians that were in service throughout the twentieth century was truly awe-inspiring. Whilst designs were refined, details rarely changed, and standard nautical fixtures including lines and rigging were comparable with those found on naval vessels as well as the overall controls. This approach made sense, given that landing craft and some amphibians, such as the LVTs, were crewed by sailors, marines or coast guards.

During the Second World War camouflage and finishing colours would depend on the theatre where the craft was operating. More often than not, these would be similar to the flotilla or squadron to which the landing craft belonged. As such, a range of camouflage patterns could be encountered which included special Admiralty colours and the US Navy's range of Measure patterns. Colours used were often taken from a palette of white, grey, blue, brown and black, whilst amphibians would be finished in a camouflage that did more to protect them on land than at sea.

Such patterns would be either single colour, normally from the US military olive green palette, or disruptive, like their landbound brethren. By the late twentieth century landing craft camouflage was changing and in the northern nations of NATO light landing craft and LCUs were appearing with a dark green and brown. The interiors were painted the same base colour as the exterior and identity markings varied from theatre to theatre.

Key points for the modeller to note are that propellers and kedge anchors are always painted, especially on amphibians, to prevent sunlight glint from bare metal surfaces whilst on land, and overall bare metal is kept to a minimum to prevent seawater

A view of the Schwimmwagen's cockpit. The layout is extremely simple and user friendly, though the bilge pump is obvious. (Three Charlie)

corrosion. As a result, bodywork damage and paintwork scuffs are attended to rapidly to prevent rusting. Pole hooks, rope fenders and splinter mattresses are all painted in the same basic colour as the vessel whilst life rings are painted in muted colours.

Landing craft ramps were lowered in a variety of ways, including cable-controlled ramps, which were controlled by a specific member of the crew, often a machine gunner. Larger landing craft such as LCMs, LCTs and LSTs featured a mix of chain-, hydraulic- and electric motor-controlled ramps. These would be controlled and deployed in a precise manner by an officer-led team, to ensure the safety of crew, passengers and vessel.

There will always be slight variations in a landing craft's or amphibian's appearance, and this depends greatly on the environment where the landing craft or amphibian is used. Whilst the equipment fitted will always be standard, colour not so much, especially after the rigours of sea crossings, weather and sun fading. This opens up a host of weathering and colouring opportunities for the modeller to explore.

Above: In contrast, the Ford GPA's cockpit is busy and slightly cramped. (Joost J. Bakker)

Right: A great view of the keel of a freshly painted Ukrainian LCU. (MoD Ukraine)

Far right: LCT1 on exercise, Inveraray, Scotland, October 1942. Note the overhead canvas cover supports and serrated deck panels to help water escape. (IWM)

Bottom: A wonderful study of the bow of a DUKW complete with rope fenders. (Alf van Beem)

Interior of an LVT-4 at the Musée des Blindés, France. (Alf van Beem)

The cavernous cargo bay of the LARC-LX. (Unknown)

A view of the rear of the DUKW. Note the painted propeller. Fort Lewis Military Museum, Washington, US. (Joe Mabel)

In Service & In Action

There is no doubt that the men who piloted the LCAs, LCVPs and LVTs in particular were exceptionally brave. They were the vanguard of an attacking force, often facing the unknown, whilst navigating unfamiliar waters, often in poor weather or at night. They would be subjected to fearsome defensive fire whilst making a landing as close as possible to an enemy shore to give the assault troops aboard their fragile craft a fighting chance. They would then return to the ship for more troops to make another journey, often up to three times.

Initial failings, often the result of poor planning, equipment management, logistical management, intelligence gathering and training, were ironed out during the early stages of the Second World War. Methods were finessed either through minor commando raids such as those in Norway (Operation Claymore) or larger assaults such as those against Dieppe (Operation Jubilee) and the Guadalcanal campaign (Operation Watchtower). But all the while lessons were being learned.

By 1943 new craft were becoming available and with them new methods of transporting men and equipment, especially from ship to shore, in the form of LVTs and DUKWs as well as the advent of pontoon causeways. This gave larger craft, such as LSTs, access to coastal points that would have simply been inaccessible beforehand.

The years of planning came to a head on the morning of 6 June 1944. Operation Overlord, of which much has been written, became the acme of the Allied amphibious warfare experience. Here resources, planning and experience met ingenuity, and the Allied assault armada that had lain in wait

Above: A loaded LCT coming alongside during exercises for the Normandy landings. (NARA)

Right: Arrival at Normandy. (Herman V. Wall)

in ports along the south coast of Great Britain landed on the beaches of Normandy far better prepared and equipped than at any other time.

By the war's end the Allies had perfected a blueprint for success in terms of assault, while, paradoxically, the Axis powers had perfected the use of landing craft as a means of evacuation on all fronts. The successful USMC landings at Inchon in the Korean War, considered a gamble even by MacArthur, was made possible by the Second World War veteran planners and Marine training staff.

Just six years later Vertical Force assets would join British and French forces for the first time, as well as UN observers for Operation Musketeer, the assault on Egyptian positions around the Suez Canal. Like Inchon before it, the military success of the operation saw a revival of broken-down French and British amphibious assets. However, these were eclipsed by the subsequent political fallout that occurred the moment British and French forces assaulted Egyptian positions.

Vietnam would witness the use of naval craft in a multitude of settings even though it was a campaign of increasing Vertical Force use. The Seventh Fleet operated a series of over-the-beach landings using its Amphibious Ready Group (ARG) to transport the USMC Special Landing Forces (SLF). The largest would be Operation Starlite, which would see 5,000 Marines land near Chu Lai, the largest city in Qu'ng Nam Province. The operation, supported by the new LVTE-1, an engineering version of the Landing Vehicle, Tracked, Personnel 5 (LVTP-5), would see the USMC establish a base at Chu Lai for the next six years.

In 1982 the Royal Navy, Royal Marines and British Army took part in Operation Corporate, otherwise known as the Falklands War. Having travelled over 8,000 miles, the invasion force made up of RN, Royal Fleet (RFA) and Ships Taken Up From Trade (STUFT) made their first uncontested landing in the style of US doctrine. This was made at San Carlos Water on 21 May 1982 using LCMs and Vertical Force assets. On 14 June, Argentine forces surrendered, bringing to a close a short but bloody war.

Even now, in the twenty-first century, the landing craft remains not only a key strategic and tactical asset but also a focal point of pride for individual crews – a more-than-worthy legacy of the pioneering days of amphibious assault in the early to mid-twentieth century.

USMC Marines and LVTs at Inchon carrying the flag given to them by Colonel Lewis B. Puller to plant at Seoul. (NARA)

An LCU dominates the background at Cua Viet as a USN LARC 5 comes ashore with a group of Marines after a run from Dong Ha. (USMC)

A British LCU from HMS *Fearless* at Ajaz Bay known as 'Red Beach', note the GPMG and gunner close to the ramp. (D. M. Gerrard)

DUKW, 470th Amphibious Truck Company, First Engineer Brigade, Utah Beach, 8 June 1944
The DUKW provided excellent logistical support in the months after the D-Day landings, especially after the destruction of the Mulberry Harbour 'A' sited at Omaha Beach on 19 June 1944. The DUKWs spent most of their time in the water, to prevent wear on their tyres, which were in short supply, dropping supplies off at the shore before heading back to the supply ship.

Rheinmetall-Borsig Landwasserschlepper, Baltic Coast, Winter, 1944
The tugboat lines of the Landwasserschlepper are clear in this series of profiles of an LWS based on the Baltic coast, where it was used for a range of tasks in shallow waters, including cargo carriage with it dedicated amphibious trailer, the Kässbohrer, which could carry up to 20 tons of stores.

Landing Craft, Mechanized (LCM) 6, United States Navy, 1960
In the watershed between the Korean and Vietnam Wars the LCM 6 provided a means of ship-to-ship liaison as well as ship-to-shore stores, troop and vehicle movements. By 1966 the LCM 6 was in use with River Flotilla 1 (RIVFLOT 1) supporting the 9th Infantry Division at Vung Tau, Vietnam. These LCMs would be converted into armoured troop carriers (ATCs) and fire support monitors.

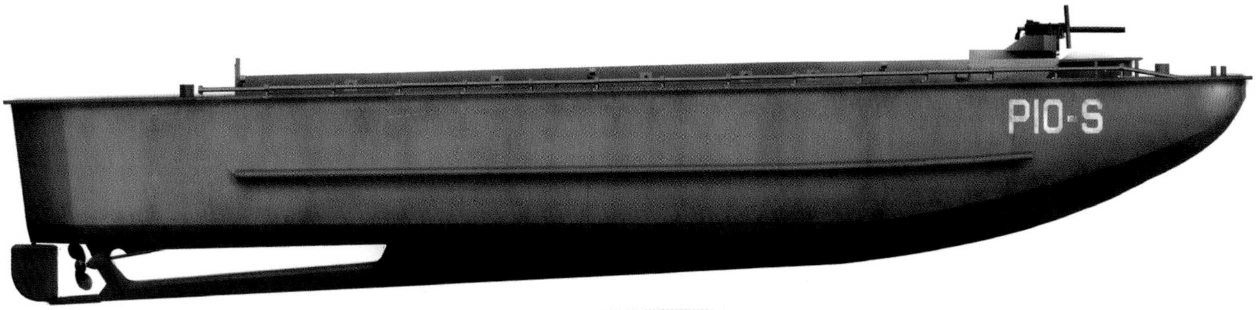

Landing Craft, Personal (Large) (LCP(L)), US Navy, Guadalcanal, August 1942
The assault on Guadalcanal was the first major offensive by US forces in the Pacific, to retake the southern Solomon Islands. As such, the LCP(L) was still very much in use even though it meant disembarking troops, up to 36, had to scramble over the bow or sides to disembark, a hazardous task in itself given the drop to the surface. The LCP(L)s would have ferried assaulting infantry between ship and shore throughout the assault, often under fire from IJN aircraft.

Landing Craft Vehicle Personnel (LCVP) *PA13-22*, US Navy, Utah Beach, 6 June 1944
The LCVP was the next generation of landing craft developed by Higgins after the LCP(L), this time featuring a bow-mounted ramp for ease of disembarkation and ensuring the safety of the 36 troops it carried. The LCVP could also carry a vehicle weighing up to 2,700kg (6,000lb) or 3,700kg (8,100lb) of general cargo. The story of *LCVP PA13-22* is particularly poignant, as just 300m from Utah Beach her bow was stuck by a single 88mm round, killing all on board and sinking her.

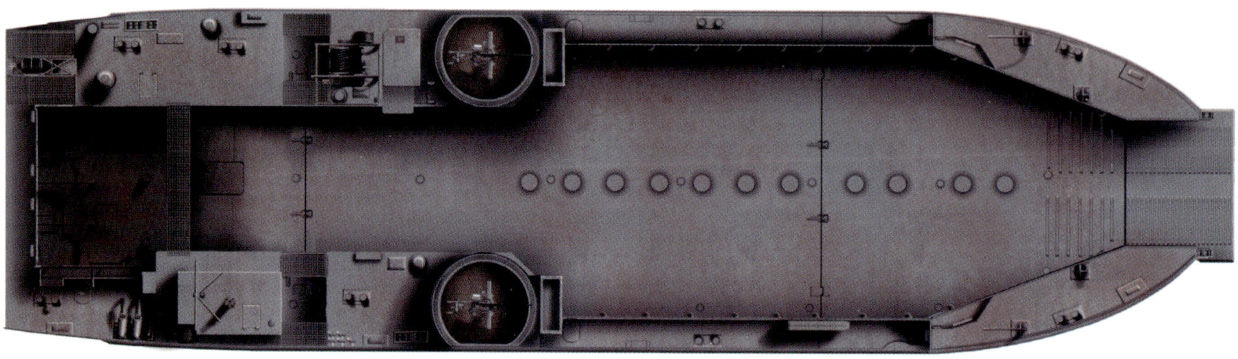

Landing Craft Tank (LCT) Mk 6, US Navy, Sea Trials, Summer 1943
LCT 501 was the first Mk 6 built with her keel being laid on 14 April 1943 by Manitowoc S. B., Manitowoc, Wisconsin. This profile shows how large the LCT class of landing craft really were. *501* ended its US career in 1959 when she was sold on to Peru.

Landing Vehicle, Tracked (LVT) 4, 2nd Marine Division, US Marine Corps, Tinian Island, 24 July 1944
Many of the islands in the South Pacific were surrounded by razor-sharp coral reefs which often damaged traditional landing craft. The LVT series of amphibians was a solution in not only getting over the reefs but also being capable of safely transporting up to 24 personnel. The LVT-4 featured a rear ramp that allowed for the safe egress of troops once their destination had been reached. Tinian Island would have a key role in the ending of the Second World War as it was where the first atom bomb, 'Little Boy', was loaded aboard the *Enola Gay*.

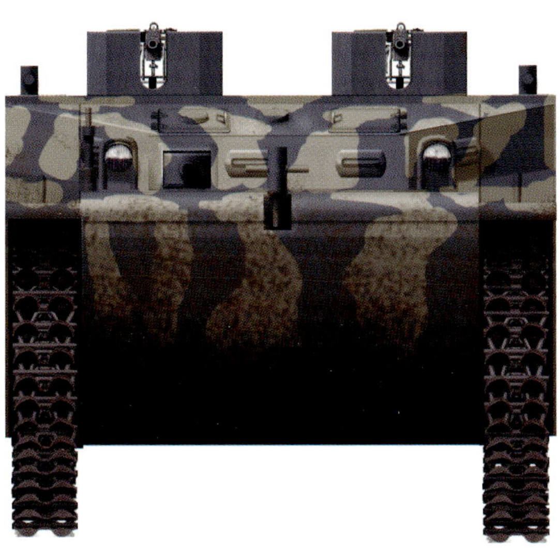

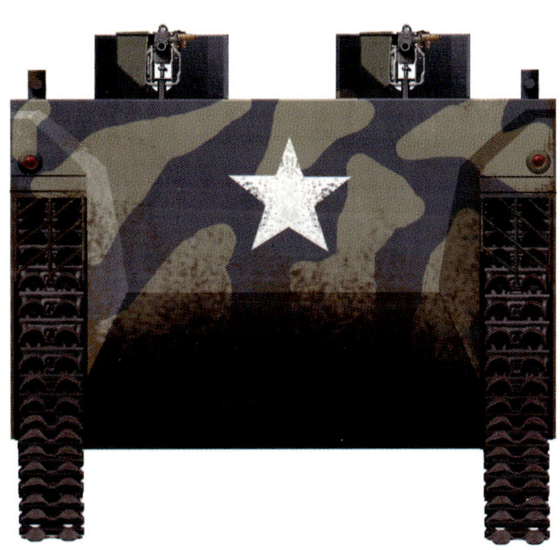

Motolance *ML 656*, I Squadriglia Pavia, 3rd Flotilla, to Maritime Department of the Upper Tyrrhenian Sea, Regia Marina, Bastia, Corsica, 11 November 1942

ML 656 was one of only nine landing craft used by the Regia Marina during the war, and given their small number, their use was somewhat limited. Interestingly these craft were crewed by workers from the very factories that built them. The MLs were then used to transport troops, 30 at a time, from the 'San Marco' Regiment, to occupy the island of Corsica. Thereafter, the 3rd Flotilla appeared not to be used again, and the craft were dispersed among the fleet, fulfilling a range of ship-to-shore tasks.

Long-established wargames' specialist Barrage Miniatures have produced a series of landing craft in 1/56 which cover those in use by both Allied and Axis forces. Their Italian Motolance ML is a wonderfully sculpted waterline model.

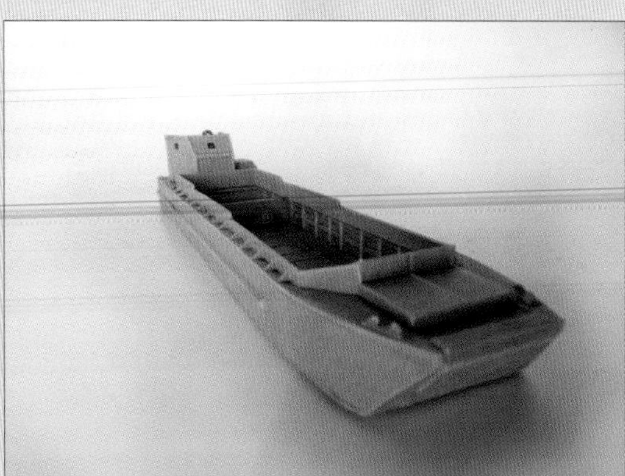

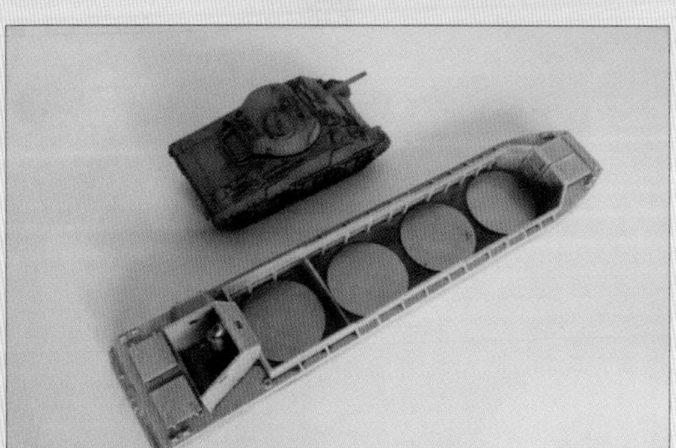

LANDING CRAFT, MECHANIZED (LCM) 3

US Navy, Rhine River crossing, March–April 1945

1/35 Scale

Brian Richardson

Italeri's 1/35 scale LCM3 was first released in 2004. It was also re-boxed by Revell in 2008 and again in 2014, replacing Dragon's US infantry figures, included with the Italeri kit, with a Jeep and trailer, another Italeri kit. The part count is quite small for this one. Starting with the hull moulded as one piece the assembly moves along quickly with a good fit all round. As with any kit there's room for improvement and new ramp pulleys have been scratch built as well as a new wheelhouse instrument panel and gun mounts (from various card and aluminium sheet metal). The model represents a weary looking LCM being prepared for the Rhine River crossing operations being brought forward on M26 Dragon wagons and painted in Olive Drab before being re-floated.

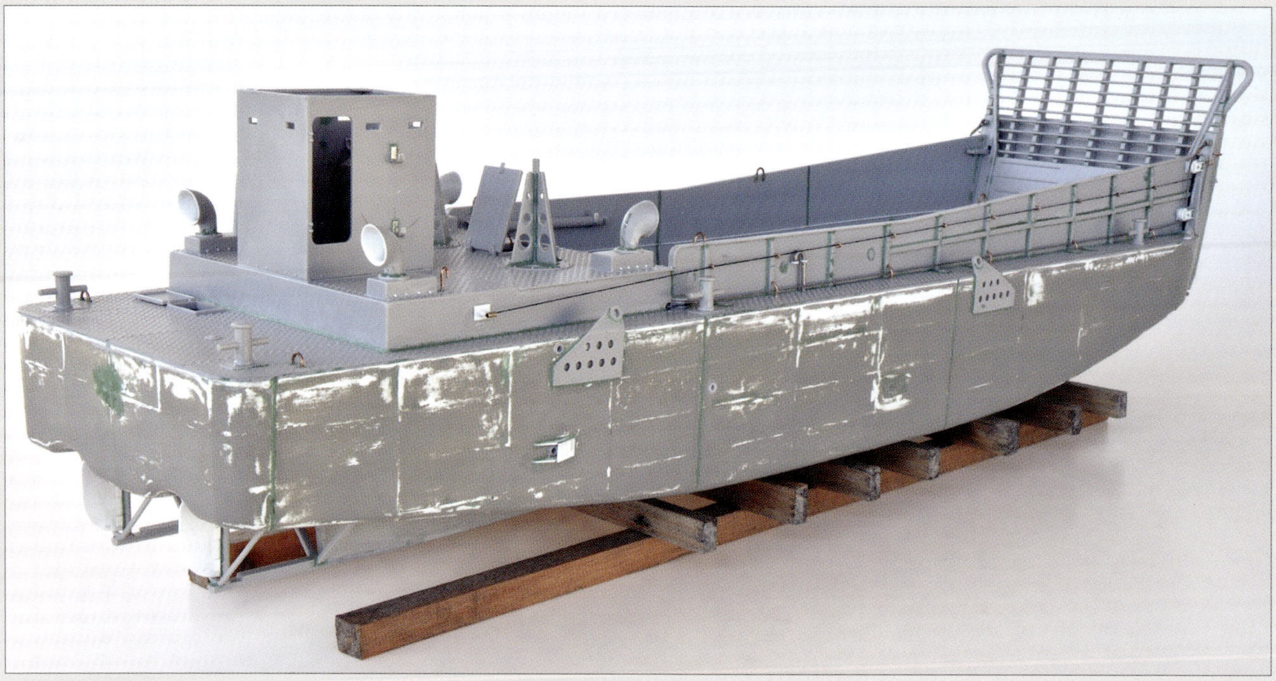

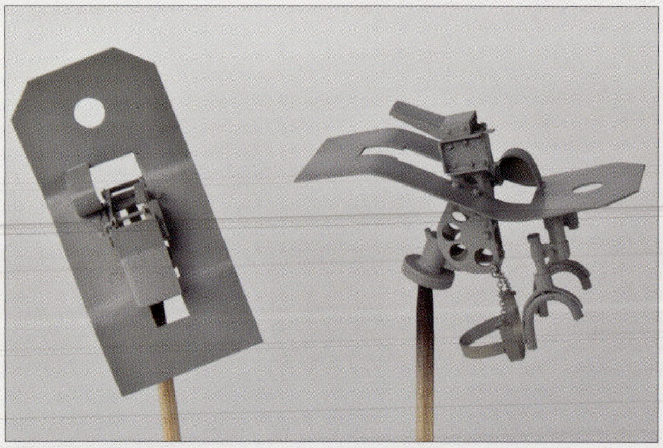

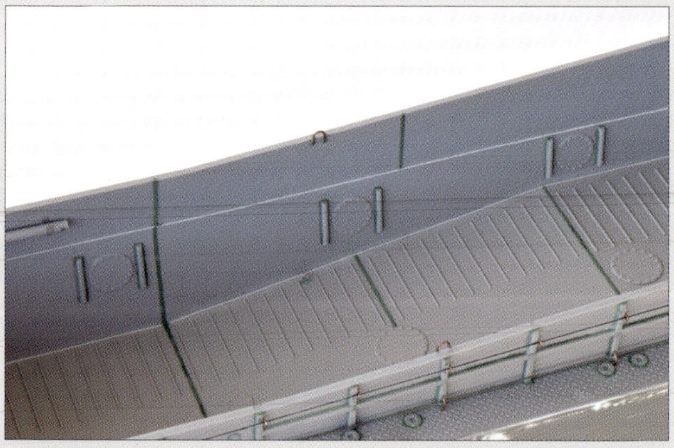

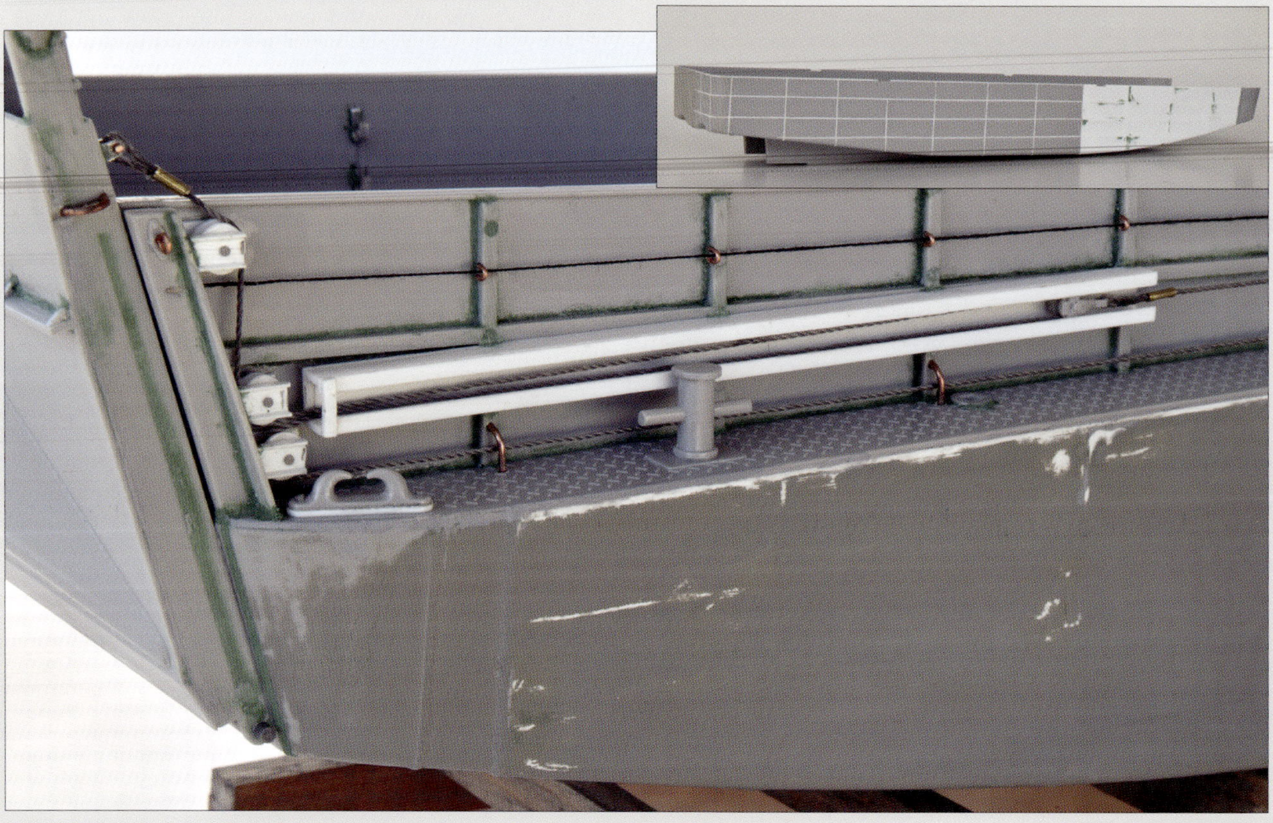

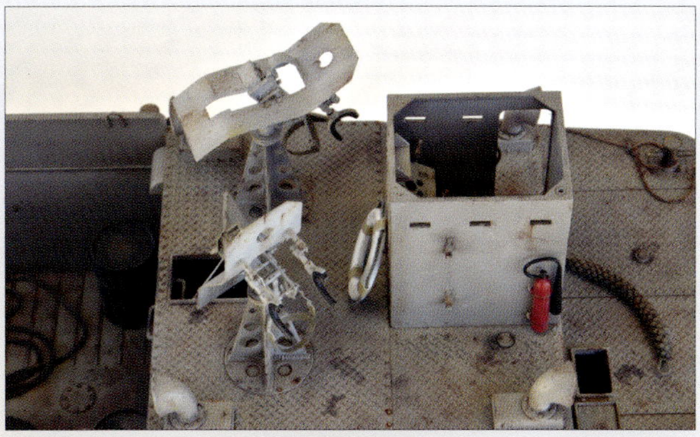

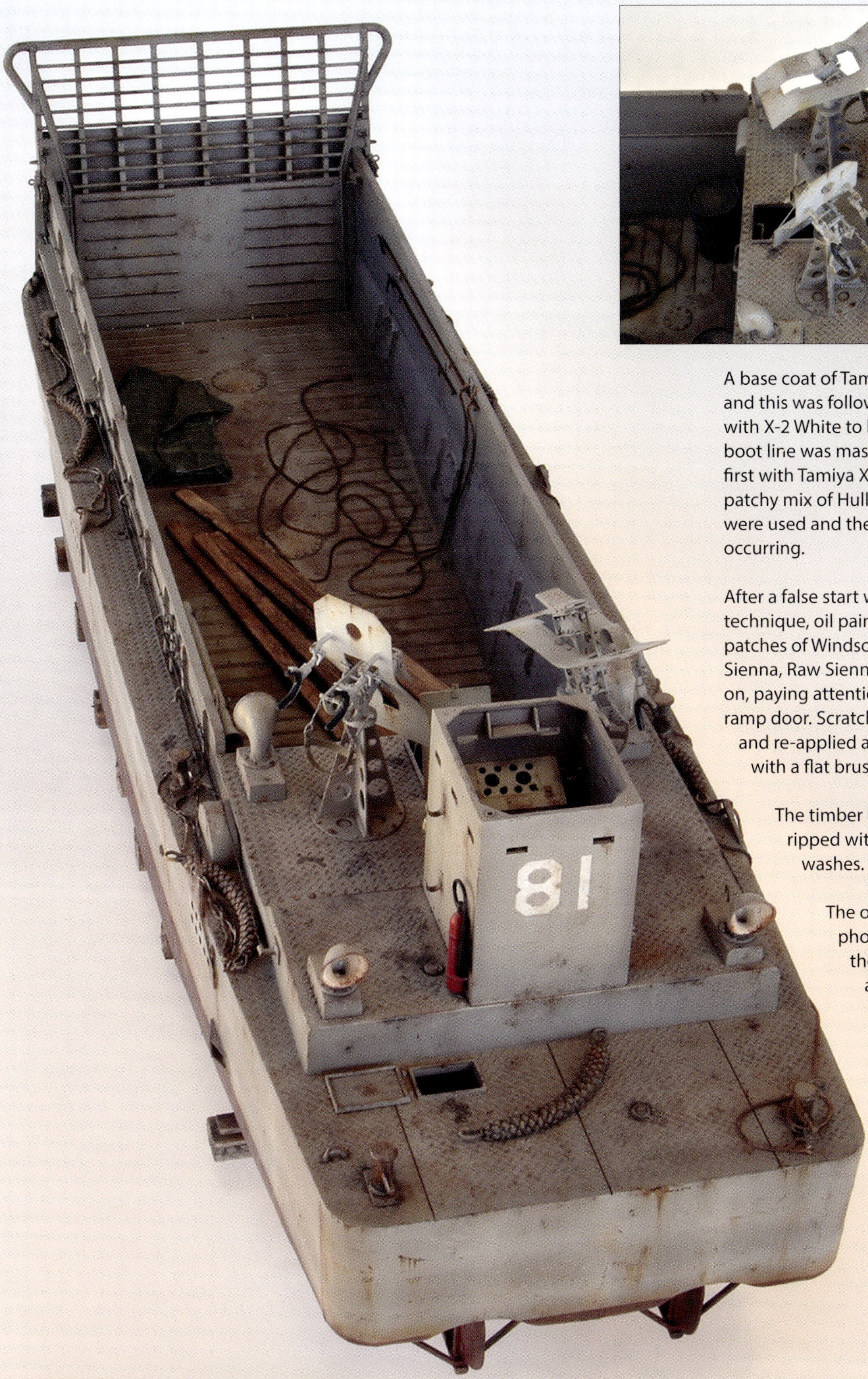

A base coat of Tamiya XF-20 Medium Grey went down and this was followed with thin lines of XF-20 lightened with X-2 White to highlight the hull and ramp ribs. The boot line was masked off and the lower hull sprayed first with Tamiya XF-9 Hull Red followed with a random patchy mix of Hull Red and X-7 Red. Italeri's decals were used and these work very well with no silvering occurring.

After a false start with a failed attempt at the hairspray technique, oil paints were resorted to and random patches of Windsor & Newton Burnt Umber, Burnt Sienna, Raw Sienna and Yellow Ochre were sponged on, paying attention to high-wear areas, especially the ramp door. Scratches were applied with a toothpick and re-applied after the oil paint was dragged down with a flat brush to create streaking.

The timber beams were made from scrap wood ripped with a circular saw and given many oil washes.

The only aftermarket used here is the photo-etch chain for the gunner's sling, the rest is card, aluminium, copper wire and solder.

The pulley and cable arrangement allows the single winch to raise and lower the ramp with a wire rope each side of the hull.

US 81
81

81 US

LANDING VEHICLE, TRACKED (LVT) 4

79th Armoured Division, Walcheren, November 1944

1/35 Scale

Brian Richardson

Italeri's LVT-4 #379 new tooling was released in 2000 and at the time was basically a good kit. Decal options are for a US Marine type and two post-war French and Italian LVTs. This model has been built to represent Sevenoaks and has been backdated to an early version by removing the bow gun and moving the assistant-driver's hatch forward. The hull shape is quite accurate, but, even if the kit is built out of the box, a couple of fixes need to be made. First, Italeri have sealed the driver's compartment roof section. The engine and transmission were moved forward to allow rear access via the ramp and the roof was bolted down on the real vehicles so this weld should be removed and replaced with bolt heads.

BISON decals BD-35013 provide enough for six LVT-4s operated by the 79th Armoured Division used in operations at Walcheren and the Rhine River crossings.

If using the kit tracks, the front drive sprocket axles aren't strong enough to take the tension and will snap off. It happens every time with this kit! An easy fix is to remove them, drill out the axles and replace them with with metal rod.

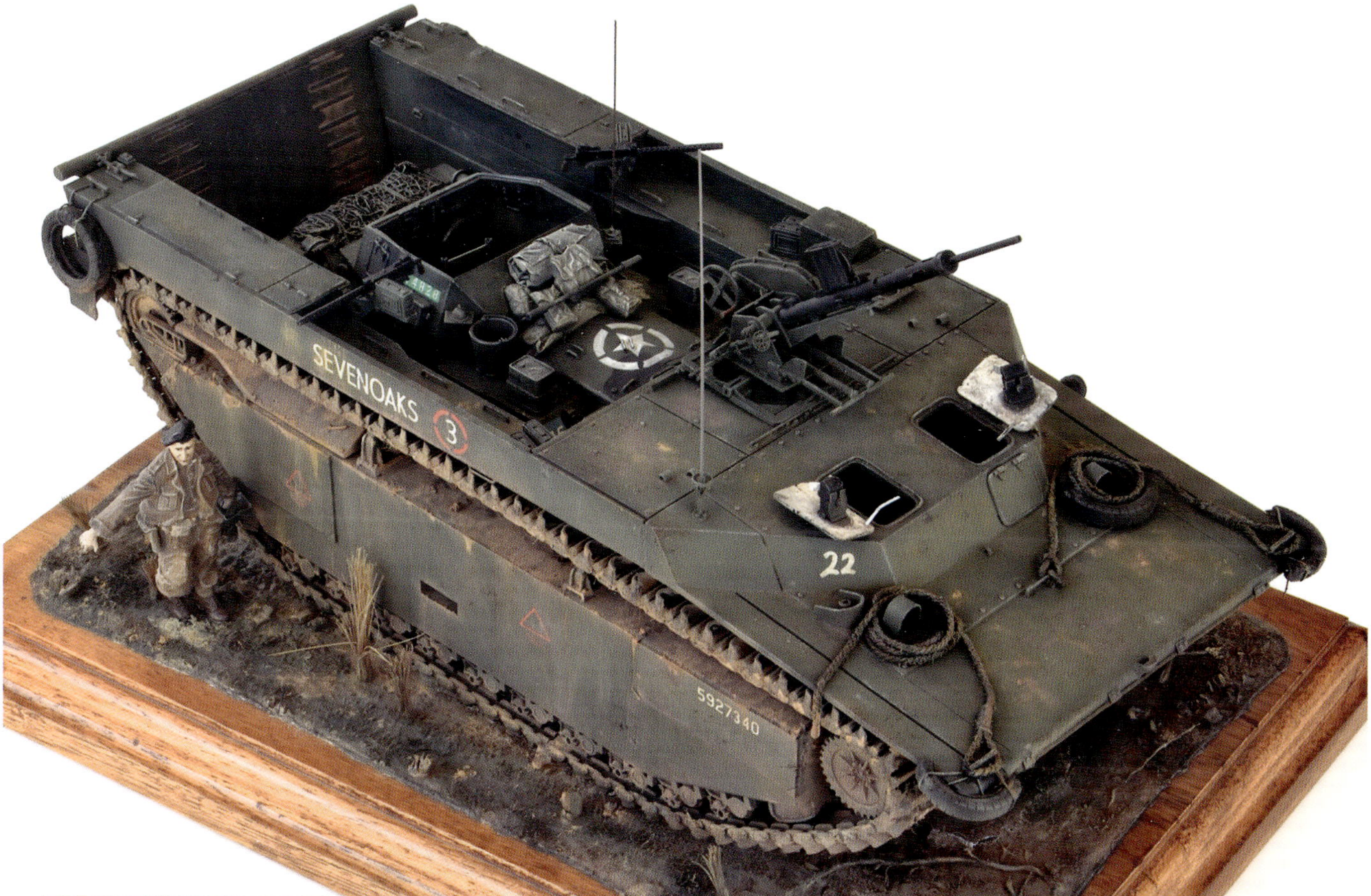

The hatches are moulded closed so quite a bit of surgery was required to open them up and make new ones. The two 30cal M1919 Browning MGs are from Academy's weapons set.

LANDING CRAFT, MECHANIZED (LCM) 8

Royal Australian Corp of Transport 1965–1967

1/35 Scale

Brian Richardson

The LCM 8 in Australian Army service was operated by the Royal Australian Corps of Transport. Eighteen were built during the mid-1960s by the North Queensland Engineers, Cairns, Queensland, Australia. The model is completely scratch built and is based on *AB 1055* as it appeared prior to 1975 when the Centurion was replaced with the West German Leopard AS1. These vessels have been used in peacekeeping missions in East Timor, Bougainville, and the Solomon Islands and have also provided commendable service during disaster relief operations. All the Australian LCM 8s are still operating and will continue to do so until at least 2027.

Two GM Detroit diesel 12V71 engines rated at 680 HP were originally fitted. These were replaced by GM 8V92 720 HP during 1998–1999 when the wheelhouse was extended and fully enclosed.

1mm Styrene sheet was mostly used, along with plastic tube, split lengthwise for the hull fenders. Other materials used include wire, brass tube various cord and string sourced from craft stores. The canopy was made from a disposable cloth hand towel. All painting was done with acrylics and hand-cut stencils.

2B
AB 1055

2B
AB 1055

FORD GPA 'SEEP'

US Army 1st Infantry Division, Tunisia, March 1943

1/35 Scale

Ben Skipper

This particular GPA has featured in a couple of photographs when it was used as a makeshift field ambulance. These provide a great insight in how the Seep was used as well as the all-important weathering aspect of the subject model in action.The Tamiya Ford GPA has its origins in a 1974 kit, which has been released three times: the original 1974 release, the 2008 release with markings for Soviet wartime use and 2014, this model, with the markings for the 1st Infantry Division. The fit is exceptional, with only a small amount of filler needed for the front where the hull top meets the bow. Even though the kit is over 45 years old, the details remain sharp, though I have augmented areas with the Eduard photo-etch (PE) set Nr. 35391. This has a host of detailing extras that can help change the kit, though I always choose the elements I use judiciously. I do find the best way to place PE onto the subject model is whilst it's still on the sprue, with the rear seat pad sides having to be trimmed to allow it to be placed past the etched sides. The model goes together quickly and smoothly. I left the wheels, seats, engine cover, windscreen, front light lenses and steering wheel to one side, ready for undercoating. The whole model received a coat of grey primer followed by Tamiya Black Green (XF-27) for the pre-shading as I felt that black would be too heavy handed. The model was then sprayed lightly with several coats of AK Interactive's Olive Drab No. 9 (AK4211). I've used this before and find that AK's paints give a good satin sheen which responds well to 1/1 thinned gloss varnish. After the first varnish coat, I applied the kit decals, which were treated to plenty of Micro Sol to help settle over the various ridges before being treated to a matt varnish finish. For weathering I referred to the photo I'd found, as well as contemporary photos of the region and noticed the region's dust is almost white, so made a suitable mix using Vallejo Beige (70.917) and White (70.951). This was then thinned and applied as several light coats before final weathering was added using brushed-on streaks. For the bilge water run-off, I used epoxy resin tinted with black oil paint. Overall a great model which is certainly as eye-catching as it is unique.

Sequence of build shots showing the great details for a model over 45 years old. The Eduard add-ons, while are not essential, just help liven up the details that little bit more.

Priming and finishing: grey primer with black green, followed by a couple of thin coats of olive drab and gloss varnish.

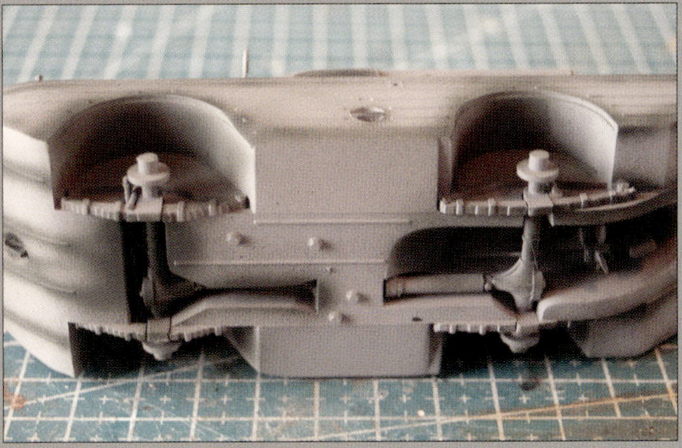

U.S.A.704020
DEVRIES

U.S.A.704020
DEVRIES

Landing craft and amphibians are extremely popular and well served by model manufacturers in all scales in a range of media. All have their merits with great potential to add multimedia detailing and conversion parts. Kits can be incorporated into both small vignettes and large-scale dioramas, especially the larger-scale landing craft. As new models are always being produced, this list is purely contemporaneous and features manufactures that are trading at the time of writing.

Kits of landing craft and amphibians have been released in numerous guises and many older models are available on auction websites. A seemingly unending range of landing craft and amphibians can be found in a range of scales from 1/700 to 1/35 with various options available to the modeller to whet the appetite.

The following scale models are currently available to purchase by modellers from their local hobby store or online, and cover the key subjects of the book.

Scale Model Kits

Italeri have produced no less than four landing craft models in 1/35 scale, three focusing on the LCVP (Nr. 6524/6441/6479) and one LCM (Nr. 6436). The 2004 moulding of the LCM features a low parts count and includes figures, both crew and disembarking infantry, who are reminiscent of early Tamiya figure sets. The mouldings are excellent, and when comparing the profile with official blueprints and contemporary line drawings, it's clear to see Italeri have done their homework with the LCM. The mouldings are sharp with the hull bottom and top being supplied as single pieces, the main cargo bay supplied as a single piece, and the ramp can be positioned open or closed. Revell have also reboxed this kit (Nr. 03000) in the past, adding a Jeep and trailer kit to provide an accessory to Italeri's LCM.

The LCVP kits are supplied with a variety of accessories. By far the most dynamic is Nr. 6524; not only does this kit come with crew but 25 multi-pose infantry figures, just short of a platoon's worth. The inclusion of the figures brings the drama of D-Day a little closer and is an excellent choice to offer the modeller. Kit Nr. 6441 is the basic LCVP, ripe for use as either a standalone piece or as part of a dynamic diorama, whilst Nr. 6479 includes the Jeep and trailer kit.

The mouldings of the LCVP kits were made in 2005 and are the same for all three LCVP kits and all four kits come with thread for the numerous ropes and lines found on the real craft. Like the LCM the part count is limited but the castings are well detailed and decals and instructions are produced to the usual high standard one expects with Italeri. Each kit is presented in a box adorned with eye-catching and dynamic artwork, making even the mundane task of reversing a Jeep and trailer seem appealing.

Regarding amphibians, Italeri have produced several models, covering mid- to late-twentieth-century subjects. In 1/35, these include the M113 ACAV (Nr. 6533), M113 ACAV with 106mm recoilless rifle (Nr. 6506), M163 VADS (Nr. 6560), the LAV 25 Piranha and Schwimmwagen (Nr. 0313). As with all Italeri kits, these are well moulded with some great details with the M113-based kits enjoying plastic tracks.

All of the kits, regardless of scale, feature wonderfully sharp decals to help finish the job. Instructions are of the usual Italeri standard with clear colour charts. In the past, Italeri have produced the DUKW and LVTs in 1/35 and 1/72 in various guises; occasionally these do appear on various bid sites demanding high resale values.

Left and below: The DUKW is very much the holy grail of model kits, but both the 1/35 and 1/72 versions are worth seeking out.

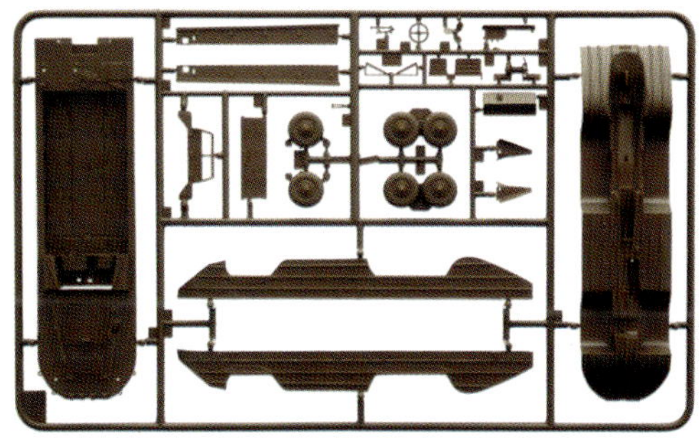

Left and below: The LAV 25 may have been a late comer in twentieth-century amphibious warfare, but the Italeri kit more than gives it justice.

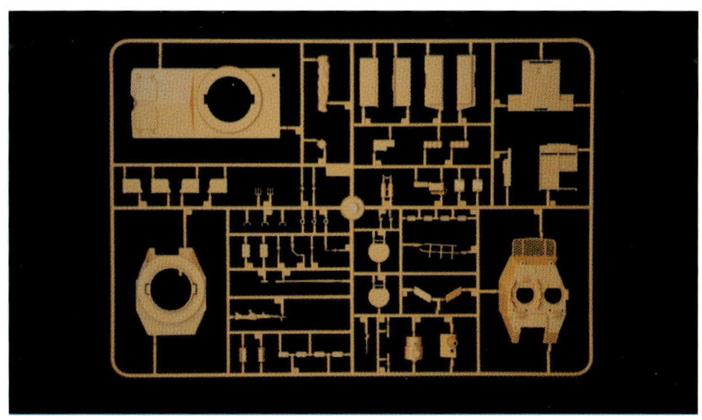

Left and below: The LCM kit is a wonderful rendition of a great landing craft and filled with possibilities too.

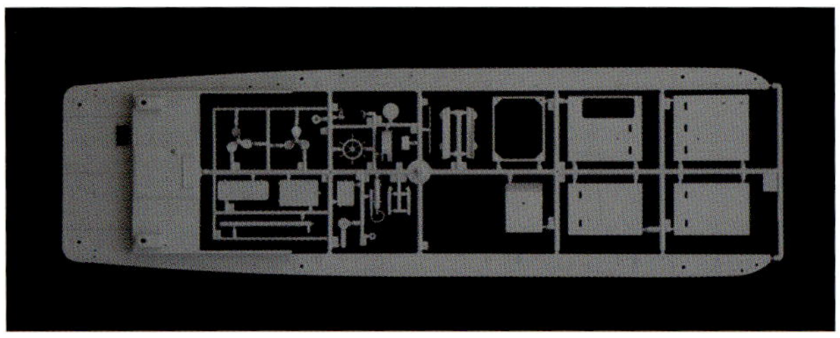

Above and left: The LCM decals offer the modeller a range of subjects. The mouldings are sharp with the hull bottom and top supplied as single pieces.

The Italeri M113 family continues to provide a great modelling experience of a fantastic subject that doesn't disappoint.

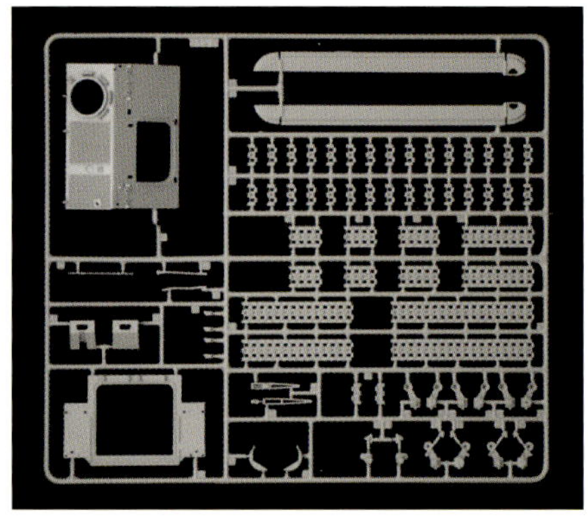

Left and all below: There's big then there's Italeri big: the LCVP is both stunning in content as it is sobering in its subject. The box art truly captures the spirit of amphibious landings.

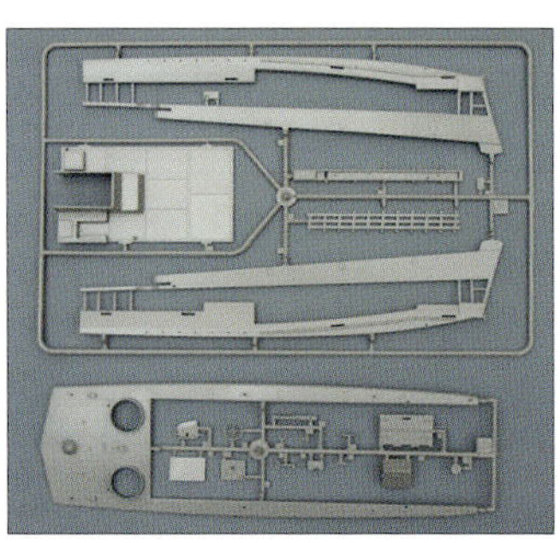

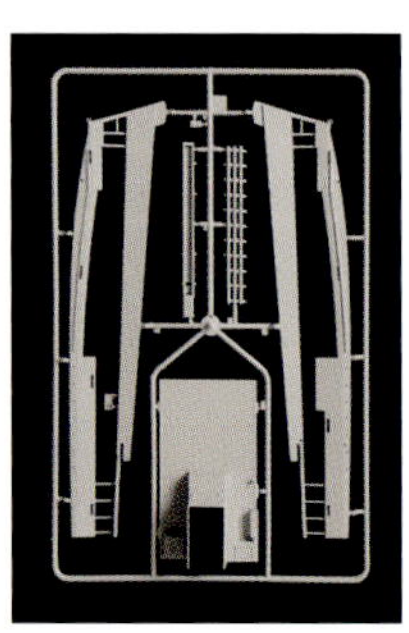

Chinese heavyweight **Trumpeter** have produced a wide range of landing craft, including the USMC (Nr. 07302) and JMSDF (Nr. 07301) LCAC in 1/72 scale. These kits feature a vinyl moulding to simulate the inflated air cushions, single-piece moulded hull and vehicle deck as well as photo-etch details. The kits also come with nine sprues of parts, some of which are delicately moulded, and gives the modeller a challenge, which is made all the easier by clear instructions and painting details. They have also produced two 1/144-scale LCACs, one in JMSDF guise (Nr. 00106) and one in USMC guise (Nr. 00107). These feature the same vinyl cushion, photo-etch fret and single-piece hull as the larger kit

Another Trumpeter 1/72 scale kit is their LCM (Nr. 07213), which features a single-piece lower hull, photo-etch fret and four sprues of parts as well as the all-important string for lines. The ramp can be positioned up or down and the all-important internal details are sharp and ready to accept a suitable load. A smaller version (Nr. 00102) in 1/144 is also available, featuring a simplified build broken down into two sprues and a moulded hull. Photo-etch and decals are sharp and in register, offering the modeller several choices of finish, and as always are presented with evocative box art. For the larger scale modeller, a 1/35 version of the LCM is also available (Nr. 00347).

For amphibians, Trumpeter have produced a simply vast range of kits including the 1/35 BMP 1D (Nr. 09572) and the BMD 3 (Nr. 09556) that feature photo-etch frets as well as separate track links, nicely produced decals and colour-sharp painting guides. Also featured

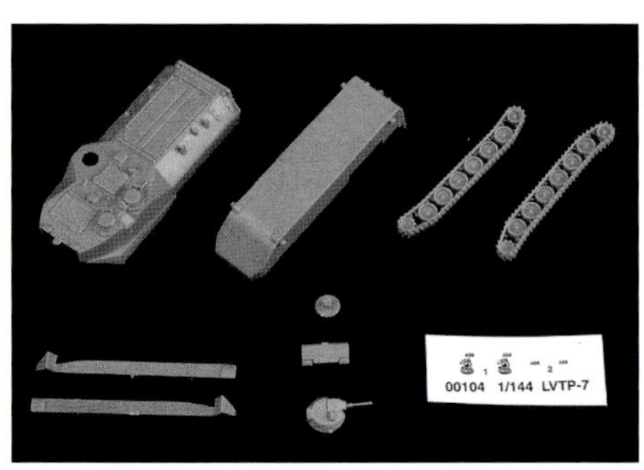

This simple kit is reminiscent of Dragon's Panzer Korps sets in terms of simplicity and detail – clearly intended to go with the 1/144 LCAC kit.

are the LVTP-7 in 1/144 (Nr .00104) and the LAV-A2 (Nr. 01521). As with most Trumpeters kits, these feature photo-etch frets, excellent instruction, clear decals and great moulding details.

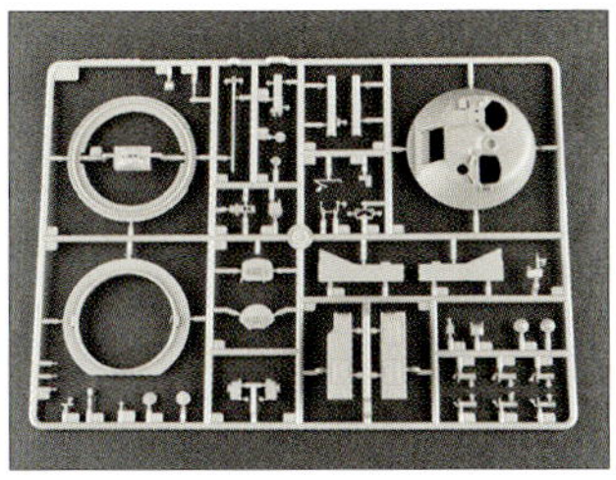

Above and below (box and decals): The BMD is one of those instantly appealing kits, helped in part by the attractive box art, clear instructions and wonderful decals.

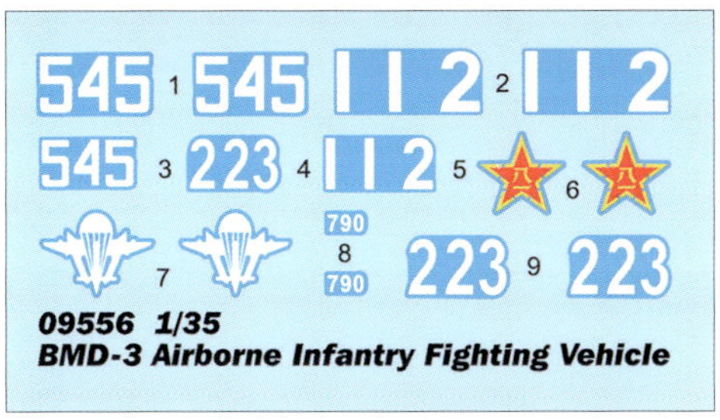

Left and below left and right: The PE frets and beautifully sculpted body will undoubtedly give the modeller hours of enjoyable modelling.

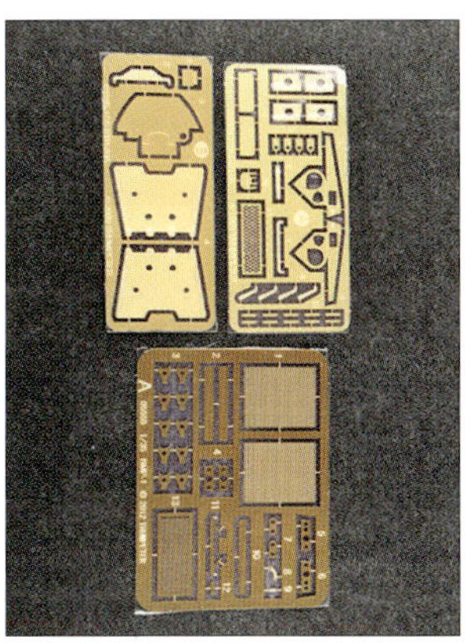

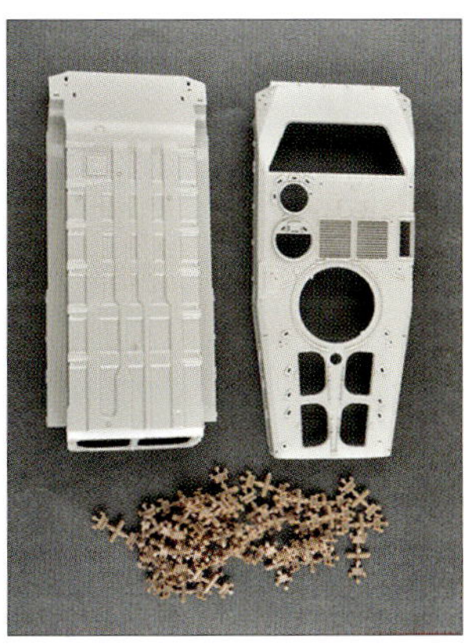

Left: The Trumpeter LAV has something of a following, and with good reason.

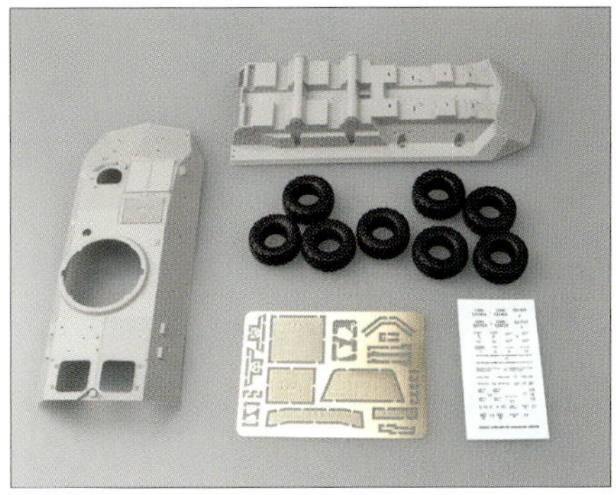

Left: Consideration should be given to replacing the Trumpeter LAV vinyl tyres with a resin set such as Def Models (Nr. DW35102).

All below: Trumpeter's LCAC model.

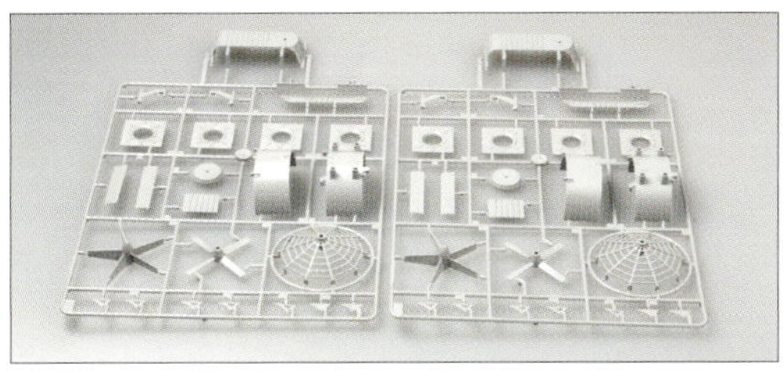

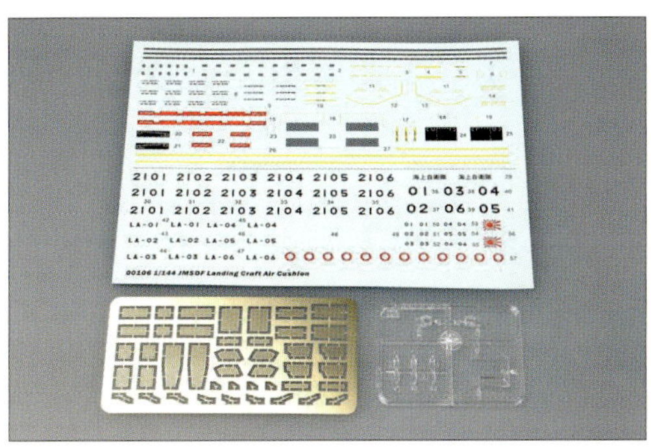

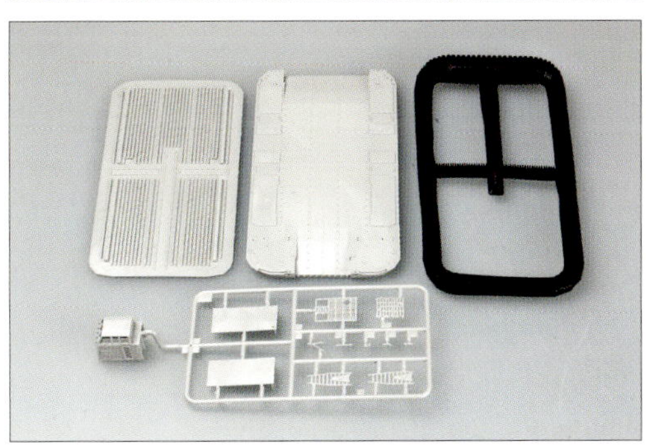

These kits wonderfully reproduce the shape of the LCM; giving the modeller three scale choices is great idea too.

Airfix has produced two distinct landing craft in the past, the LCM3 (Nr. A03301V) and the Heller-based LCVP (Nr. A02340). In 2014, Airfix produced their own LCVP, whilst Heller continued to produce their version in parallel. The Airfix kits benefit from CAD-enhanced features in the initial design period and the kits are an improvement on the Heller offering. The Airfix LCVP is presented in an attractive box, packed with details, though there are a couple of areas that need fettling, such as the mooring bollards, which are represented as protruding rectangles. The decals are sharp and the new-style instructions provide a clear step-by-step process without ambiguity, which sometime crept in with the earlier Airfix instructions.

The dramatic box art of the Heller kit belies the fact the kit lacks a little of the finesse of both the Trumpeter and new Airfix kits but still includes details such as thread for lines and decals that provide the modeller with the option to build various versions. The moulding is still sharp enough to render a good model, but this is dulled somewhat by the softer plastic in which it's moulded. As well as the standard LCVP kit, there is also a starter kit featuring paints and glue (Nr. 56995).

This kit can still hold a light against more contemporary offerings and the inclusion of figures will pique many modellers' interest.

Instructions are a little crammed, and the lack of a plan view of the finished kit to help with painting and decals is disappointing.

Airfix's LCM and Sherman kit is fast approaching its 60th anniversary and the fact it's still in production as part of the new Vintage Classics range speaks volumes about the kit's appeal. Both elements of the kit are of their time, and are intended to be made as a nostalgic experience as opposed to being of the sharper-styled kits produced by a host of companies. Even so, combined, they present the modeller with a great opportunity to produce a diorama from a box. The decals are provided for only one example each of the LCM and Sherman, though after-market decals and some inventive use of the craft knife will produce a few variations.

Also joining the LCM3 in the Vintage Classics range is the Buffalo LVT IV (Nr. A02302V) and Willys Jeep combo and the DUKW (Nr. A02316V). Again, these kits whose heritage harks back to the golden age of mid-twentieth-century modelling, presenting even the most discerning modeller with a welcome break or challenge. All three of these Vintage Classics kits come with the original instructions, which can be challenging on first inspection as they can be visually cluttered. That said, Airfix have provided the modeller with wonderfully clear colour charts to help finish the kits.

All box art to the left: The return of the action-packed box art makes these Vintage Classics kits as attractive as when first released 60 years ago. The LCVP is all new and shows how far Airfix have come over the past decade.

Airfix LCVP.

Academy have built up an enviable reputation producing models of exceptional quality and value, so much so that Airfix have started to re-box some of their Second World War armour. However, their offerings to amphibians is centred around their fine M113 family of kits, the ACAV (Nr. 13266) and the M163 (Nr. 13507). The models are always beautifully cast though occasionally the odd sink mark can appear in an awkward position. Instructions have improved over time, but occasionally decals can be fragile, though the colours are always strong.

AFV Club, and their Hobby Fan range of resin models, have produced several kits for the modeller which include 1/350 LSTs (Nr. PKSE73515 and PKSE73519), and a set of 1/350 vehicles (Nr. PKSE73516), while Hobby Fan have produced a base for the LSTs in resin (Nr. PKHF094). The LST is a fantastic kit awash with details, a nice touch being the dimpling of the stressed skin of the hull sides as well as LCMs awaiting deployment in their davits. Also included is a range of vehicles, including an LVT, which can be supplemented by Nr. PKSE73516. An LCT Mk 6 (Nr. SE73518) is also available as a 1/350 kit, which includes two LCTs as well as a couple of vehicles, including an M245 Chaffee.

Both are relatively new releases, the LST released in 2018 with the LCT following in 2019. Detailing is exceptional and the instructions, complete with colour guides, are well laid out and easy to follow. Decals are sharp and reflect the blocky type used by the USN beautifully. AFV Club also produce photo-etch sets for both craft, AG35050 for the LST and AG35052 for the LCT.

For the larger-scale modeller AFV Club also produce the M113 in various guises whilst Hobby Fan have produced a wonderfully detailed mixed media resin-based kit of the LARC-LX in 1/72 (HF077). This is joined by an early LARC-V (HF072), as well as the open-topped M778 Amphibious Assault Armoured Vehicle (HF075) that was used exclusively by the USMC, predominantly in Vietnam. Hobby Fan have also produced the M778's predecessor, the M116 Husky (HF073) and the M113 (HF022).

AFV Club have also produced the LVTP-7 (AF35S67), LVTP5 (AF35022) and LVT-4 (AF35205), the latter of which is awash with fine details, including driver's compartment and ramp. The construction of the LVT-4 is, as you might expect, complex but the instructions guide you through each stage clearly. For the Second World War modeller AFV Club have also produced a Schwimmwagen (AF35228) which features vinyl tyres and photo-etch extras.

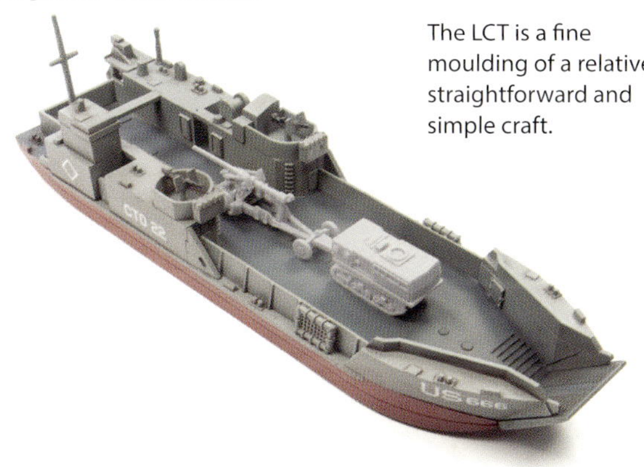

The LCT is a fine moulding of a relatively straightforward and simple craft.

Above and below: AFV Club's LST is astounding with amazing attention to detail that certainly entices even the most reticent modeller to try their hand at maritime modelling.

The LARC-LX is certainly an imposing-looking beast out of the water …

The Schwimmwagen is nicely observed and certainly holds its own as a straightforward kit.

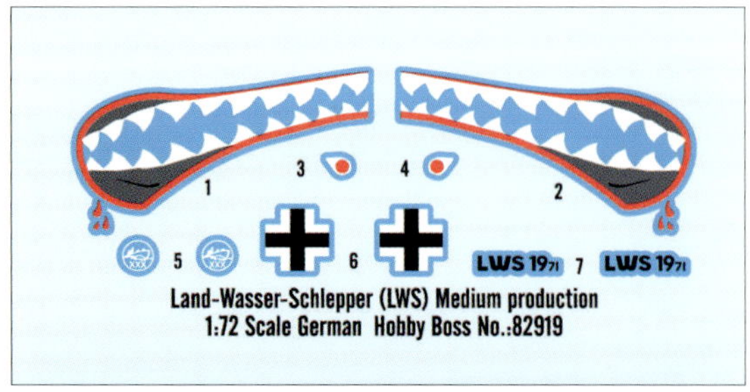

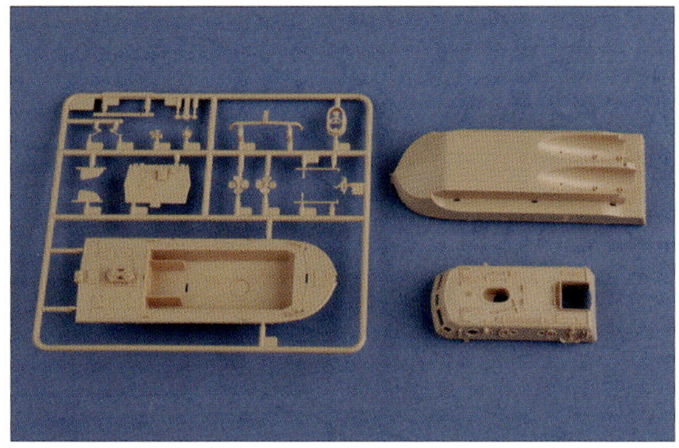

The Hobby Boss Landwasserschlepper is a wonderfully detailed and straightforward little kit.

Bronco models, like many of the large manufacturers, have built up an enviable range of model kits since 2010. For the 1/35 modeller they offer the early Landwasserschlepper (LWS) (Nr. CB35031), mid-term production version (Nr. CB35015) and a slightly later version (Nr. CB35020). The kits feature beautifully moulded parts, including a two-piece hull, plastic tracks and a set of suitably themed nautical accessories, including rope fenders for the later version. Also included in the Bronco range is a 1/350 AAVTP7A1 (Nr. NB5036) for those wanting to build post-war dioramas.

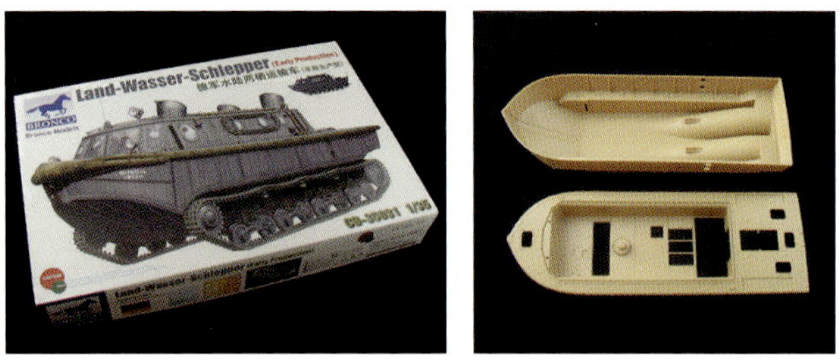

Bronco's Landwasserschlepper are certainly head-turning kits of one of the more unusual Second World War amphibians.

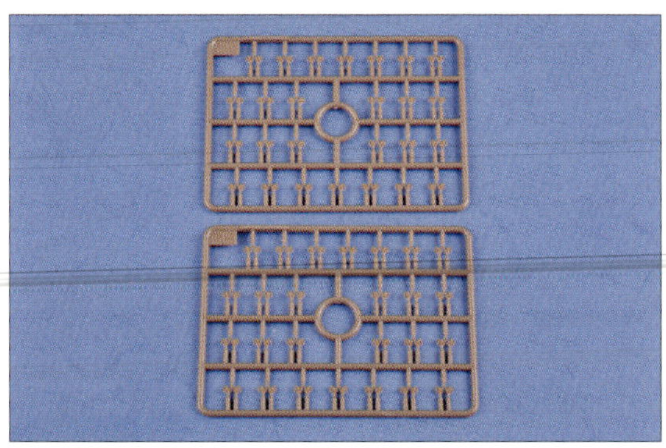

In the past **Dragon** have produced a range of landing craft and amphibians; their current catalogue includes the 1/72 LCM3 and Sherman as well as a transparent base (Nr. 7516). Dragon have also produced various versions in 1/72 (Nr. 7509) and 1/35 (Nr. 6669) of the Landwasserschlepper (LWS) Prototype Nr. II which was built around the Panzer IV chassis. As always, the kits are extremely well detailed, if not a little too much so, but certainly make for an interesting subject. For Allied equipment Dragon produced the LVT, again in 1/35 (Nr. 9134) and 1/72 scales (Nr. 7388), as well as a pre-built 1/6 Schwimmwagen (Nr. 75013) for the larger-scale modeller. Whilst Dragon kits are always beautifully produced, the instructions can always be improved and it's suggested that any modeller embarking on making a Dragon kit does so with caution, checking part numbers and procedures. Decals are always a strong point though and these won't leave you disappointed.

Hobby Boss have produced a range of amphibians from Second World War: the Landwasserschlepper in 1/72 (Nr. 82919) and 1/35 (Nr. 824030) as well as

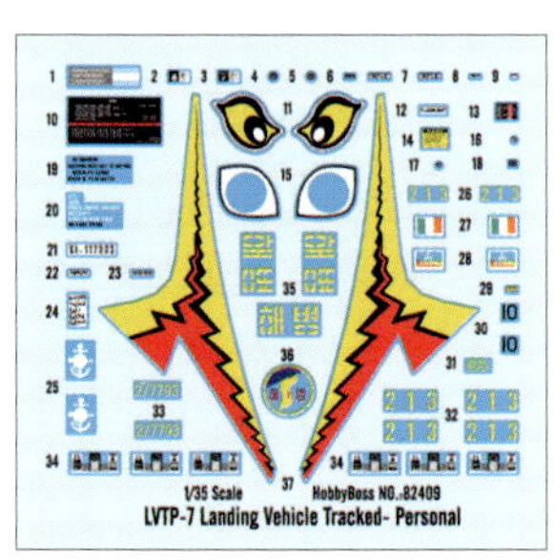

The T-40's potential was cut short by war, but even so this kit is a great addition to any modeller's stash. The early LAV is presented in a wonderful box containing a finely detail miniature replica of the real vehicle. The LVTP-7 would easily take pride of place on any modeller's shelf, or as part of a themed diorama.

the T-40 (Nr. 83826) in 1/35, which features plastic tracks. Cold War vehicles include the LAV-150 APC in 1/35 (Nr. 82421) and the LVTP-7 (Nr. 82409). These are present in boxes finished with stunning artwork and the mouldings are always of exceptional quality. Decals are sharp and true to register, while instruction are visually clear, though the steps in each stage are often quite involved and so are worth paying extra attention too.

Tamiya's offering of amphibians is restricted to the Ford GPA (Nr. 35336), which features in the showcase build section, and the Schwimmwagen (Nr. 35003), which is the model that was originally released in 1970. The Schwimmwagen was subject to a retool as the Type 166 (Nr. 35224) in 2008 and re-released in 2014. The later of the two kits offers more detail, but the currently available version certain taps into the vintage kit's realm, which is increasing in popularity. The Schwimmwagen is also available as a 1/48-scale kit, Nr. 32506. For the post-war modeller there remains Tamiya's fine collection of M113 vehicles centred on the 1974 release of kit Nr. 35040.

Tamiya have also produced a wonderful 1/700 waterline Japanese Military Transport Set, Nr. 31501, which features two Second World War vessels, including a 101-class landing ship. All kits are beautifully presented, with the 1/35 version coming with figures, giving the modeller some great options. The kits themselves are well engineered and are treated to Tamiya's enviable instructions and exceptional decals. Whilst the kits are older than most, there are numerous add-ons available to bring these venerable kits up to date.

Japanese manufacturer **Pit Road** produce predominantly IJN subjects, and have produced two 1/350 kits of landing ships, the Class 101 (WB05) and Class 103. Both kits come complete with a range of accessories including the Type 2 Ka-Mi, and Dai Hatsu landing craft. For the super detailers there is also a Class 103 complete with nameplate and printed photo-etch set (WB07). For the post-war modeller there is also an LCAC in 1/144 complete with Type 10 tank and photo-etched details and a bridge interior.

Tamiya's almost vintage Schwimmwagen and Ford GPA kits are still worthy of consideration, and with so many fine-tuning options available from third parties such as Eduard, the possibilities are endless.

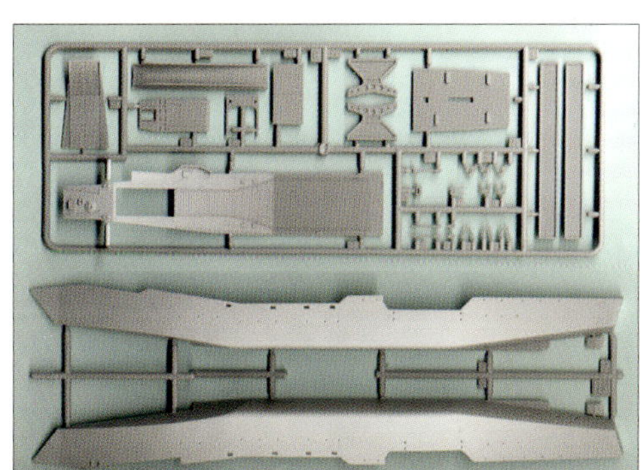

Pin Roads Class 101 is a fine kit of an unusual subject, but is well worth consideration as a side project.

There is a host of resin models and detailing options in a range of scales which include **Schatton Modellbau** who have produced a mixed media 1/35 Wehrmacht Pioneer (PilaBo) landing craft 39 (Nr. 3584). Similar in size to an LCVP, this kit opens up a world of possibilities for the modeller. The main elements are cast in resin with multimedia details and the design allows the PilaBo to be modelled with its clamshell bow doors open and the ramp deployed. The model is also capable of carrying a scale model of any vehicle up to the size of the Sd.Kfz. 7, which makes for interesting diorama and vignette options.

French resin and photo-etch masters **Master Piece Models** have produced amphibians in 1/48 scale, including the DUKW, as well a 1/35 Armoured Troop Carrier (ATC), a converted LCM used during the Vietnam War, which features a helicopter landing deck (Nr. MMVN002).

Belgian-based resin casters **Resicast** have built up a sound reputation over the years and have included in their range a beautifully sculpted 1/35 resin and photo-etch Terrapin (Nr. 351210). This is joined by a Sherman BARV conversion kit (Nr. 351126).

Terrapin and BARV are great for inclusion in Second World War dioramas focusing on late 1944 Northern Europe.

Another producer of resin and photo-etch landing craft are American manufacturers **Iron Shipwrights** who offer the modeller a series of LCIs, as well as a superb LCS(L) kit in 1/350.

For those modelling in miniature, **Milicast** offer the a crisply cast Terrapin in 1/76 (Nr. UK209); also featured is the DUKW (Nr. US144) which can be supplemented with bespoke British D-Day decals (DTM-T-76045). Other kits include the Sherman and later Centurion BARVs. A full range of LVTs is also available.

Milicast then gives the modeller a great selection of landing craft modelling options, both British and American. These are simply exquisite and are available as full hull or waterline craft. These include LCIs (Nr. LCILUK), LCAs (Nr. LCA), LCMs (Nr. LCM3W) and LCTs (Nr. LCT(5)). All kits are a mix of resin and photo-etch and as breathtaking in their scope as they are in their detail.

Scottish resin masters Accurate Armour have produced three resin landing craft kits in 1/76. All are superbly detailed waterline kits. The British-made LCT (4) (Nr. S13) is the first of the three kits, which is as impressive in size as it is in detail.

Accurate Armour's LCF (4) (Nr.S17), based on the LCT (4), kit is awash with details. The guns are beautifully cast in resin and are supplemented with some delicate photo-etch details.

Above and below: The Accurate Armour LCT (5) (NrS18) is a US-based LCT and features markings for both Royal Navy and USN craft and enjoys the same attention to detail as the LCT (4) .